DISCLAIMER OF WARRANTY/LIMIT OF LIABILITY

A PRAYER FOR THE IRS

Oh, Internal Revenue Service,
ruler of all Washington,
We sanctify thee, as thou
goest about thy business,
enthroned by the glory of Congress
and the powers of section 7801 of the
Internal Revenue Code.

Have mercy on thy servants,
oh mighty Department of the Treasury,
and forgive us our hallowed deductions.
Deliver us from the grasp of the statutory
authority of the revenue auditor,
and lead us into the promised land
of the everlasting refund.

INTRODUCTION

Not too long ago, a client of mine that has several years of un-filed taxes called me up with glee in his voice. "I found all my records," he said. "Now we can begin!" "Bring 'em over," I yelled. After all, we're still trying to get 2002 filed and hope to get 2005 done before I retire. Later on that day I looked out my office window and there he was, unloading a file cabinet from the back of his pickup truck, papers swirling in the breeze. Well, I thought, at least there's a filing system. After dropping the cabinet in the middle of my office, he triumphantly pulled open the drawer. Oh yeah, we had records, thousands of them, and they exploded into the room.

The strange thing is, I love this stuff. I've been a tax preparer for 27 years and I imagine that I'll probably do it for another 27. I love it because it's so much fun to pull out of a client everything I need to know to make their tax returns work for them. The frustrating part for most people is that they don't imagine what deductions are out there. Finding information in the thousands of pages of tax code and instructions is just not fun.

So, here we have A to Z™ FOR HOME OFFICE & SELF-EMPLOYED which cuts through the tax code technicalities. It's a simple, alphabetized listing of the deductions that may be available to those with home offices and the self-employed. You'd be surprised how much you can save if you itemize your tax deductions. And no, itemizing deductions on your tax return does not trigger an audit. You must keep the proper records, though!

Our first challenge is to get through the language of the IRS. Adjusted Gross Income is important because it is used for calculating many of the deductions you'll be taking for medical expenses, charitable contributions, interest, casualty losses, and miscellaneous expenses. Adjusted Gross Income (AGI) starts with the total of your income from many possible sources (wages, unemployment compensation, gains or losses from the sale of assets, rents collected, royalties, alimony received, and some Social Security benefits). Add that all together and then reduce that number by some specific adjustments.

Adjustments can include retirement contributions, alimony payments, allowable student loan interest and tuition payments, and moving expenses. There are additional adjustments available for specific types of taxpayers, such as business owners and schoolteachers. The remaining income is your AGI. This is the number you write at the bottom of page 1 of your 1040 form, and then again at the top of page 2.

Here's how to compute your AGI:

Sources of Income:

Wages, including salary, tips, bonuses	$100,000
Interest income and dividends	2,500
State tax refunds	525
Alimony received	24,000
Business income	3,500
Capital gains or losses	(3,000)
Unemployment compensation	8,000
Taxable, IRA, pension or annuity distribution	1,500
Rental real estate, partnership income, etc.	1,350
Taxable Social Security benefits	-0-
Other income	-0-
Total Income	**$138,375**

Less Adjustments

Educator expenses	$250
Certain business expenses of reservists, performing artists, etc.	1,000
Health savings account deductions	0
Moving expenses	0
Self-employment tax	47
SEP, SIMPLE, and qualified plans	691
Self-employed health insurance deduction	3,453
Penalty on early withdrawal of savings	0
Alimony paid	0
IRA deduction	0
Student loan interest deduction	172
Tuition and fees deduction	2,000
Other deductions	0
Total Adjustments	**$7,613**

Adjusted Gross Income **$130,762**

Of course when dealing with the tax code, nothing is simple. It's possible that the total amount of your itemized deductions may be limited. If your AGI exceeds a predetermined amount ($145,950 for single and married taxpayers, $72,975 for married taxpayers filing separate returns in 2005) then the amount of your total allowable itemized deductions will be reduced by 3% of the difference between your AGI and the predetermined amount for that year.

And there's also something called Modified Adjusted Gross Income (MAGI) which the IRS uses in place of AGI to calculate certain deductions. Generally, this is your regular AGI plus or minus various tax credits, deductions, and specific categories of income that were excluded or exempted from your AGI calculation. These can include foreign income, student loan deductions, IRA contribution deductions, and deductions for higher education costs. The precise additions or subtractions applied to AGI to reach MAGI will vary by credit or deduction category.

Throughout the book there are references to different expense thresholds, each based on a percentage of adjusted gross income: 2% for miscellaneous expenses; 7.5% for medical expenses; and 10% for casualty losses. When you see a reference to an expense threshold, it means that the deductibility of that expense is limited by an amount derived from the threshold rate.

For example, to determine your medical deduction, you have to start with your AGI. Using the example above, with an AGI of $130,762, your AGI threshold (7.5% of $130,762) would be $9,807. That means you can deduct all qualified medical expenses that exceed $9,807.

Most miscellaneous deductions are deductible after subtracting only 2% of adjusted gross income. Personal deductions may be limited, but the IRS has been very generous in allowing deductions for almost every type of revenue-producing activity once you reach that threshold.

My hope is that as you look through the book, you'll see deductions available to you that you never knew about. Once you have identified the potential deductions that apply to you, you may want to start keeping track of your expenses. There is one certainty I have observed over the years, and that is that there's a direct correlation between the tax dollars that you can save and the quality of your record keeping. This book includes sample record keeping logs that show you how to keep track of some of the most common deductions, such as automobile expenses, travel expenses, and charitable donations. There is also a separate log book, A to Z™ LOG BOOK that is great for your briefcase or glove compartment. Trust me, your tax preparer will thank you!

What this book does not tell you is how to file your taxes or how to do tax planning. For that, I advise you to see a certified tax planner, tax attorney, or certified public accountant. There are also some terrific do-it-yourself software programs available. Many of my clients use them to organize their tax information before coming to my office.

In many cases your trade, profession, employment status, or other circumstances can change your tax status, making you eligible for tax deductions that are unique. More specialized discussions of the deduction criteria for certain taxpayers and listings of deductions that are distinctive to certain taxpayer groups can be found in other A to Z™ titles that focus on members of the clergy; writers, artists and performers; educators; sales professionals; health care professionals; trades people and union members; people who have home offices; the self- employed; as well as other types of taxpayers.

As for what to keep and what to throw away, I think of it this way: You must keep your records for as long as they are needed to support your tax filings and until the statute of limitations for that return runs out. The statute of limitations is the period of time in which you can amend your return to claim a credit or a refund, or the IRS can assess additional tax.

If your tax returns are not fraudulent or un-filed, or your income is not understated by more that 25%, you can discard most of your records seven years from the filing date of the return. You must also retain records relating to a claim on worthless securities for seven years.

There is no statute of limitations on un-filed or fraudulent returns. A document retention guide can be found in the back of this book.

Believe it or not, I tell my clients all the time, this is fun stuff! Hopefully, this book will put a smile on your face, an extra penny in your pocket, and make your next tax season the best ever.

Enjoy!

Anne Skalka

Anne Skalka, CPA

A

ACCIDENT *See Casualty Loss*

The cost of damage to your home, car, or personal property due to an accident is tax deductible. The loss is first reduced by applicable proceeds from insurance or relief agencies. The first $100 of the net loss is nondeductible. The balance of the loss in excess of 10% of your adjusted gross income (AGI) may be deducted. Self-employed individuals can deduct the net loss on business property directly from adjusted gross income without first reducing the loss by 10%. If the damage is to property used for both business and personal purposes, a portion of the loss can be allocated to the home office based on the percentage of your home used for business.

ACCIDENT INSURANCE

Accident insurance premiums are tax deductible as a medical expense. Medical expenses can be deducted after they have reached the required threshold of 7.5% of your AGI. Business-related accident insurance is fully deductible for self-employed individuals.

ACCOUNTANT *See Tax Preparation*

Accountant fees associated with the preparation, filing, and auditing of both your federal and state tax returns are tax deductible. These accountant fees are categorized as a miscellaneous expense, subject to the 2% AGI threshold. For self-employed individuals, accountant fees associated with your business are treated as a business expense, deducted directly from self-employment income.

ACUPUNCTURE *See Medical Expense*

Acupuncture can be deducted as a medical expense if it is doctor-prescribed to treat a specific medical condition. Acupuncture treatments to improve your general health and well-being are not tax deductible. Qualified medical expenses are tax deductible after reaching the required threshold of 7.5% of your AGI.

ADJUSTED GROSS INCOME (AGI)

Your adjusted gross income (AGI) is used as the basis for calculating expense thresholds as you itemize your allowable tax deductions for medical expenses, charitable contributions, interest, casualty losses, and miscellaneous expenses. (See Introduction)

Adjusted gross income (AGI) is the number you write at the bottom of page 1 of your 1040 form, and then copy again at the top of page 2.

Adjusted gross income (AGI) starts with the total of your income from many possible sources (wages, unemployment compensation, gains or losses from the sale of assets, rents collected, royalties, alimony received, and some Social Security benefits). Add those together and then reduce that number by some specific adjustments.

Adjustments can include retirement contributions, alimony payments, allowable student loan interest and tuition payments, and moving expenses.

There are additional adjustments available for specific categories of taxpayers, such as business owners and school teachers. The remaining income, after it has been reduced by these adjustments, is your AGI.

ADOPTION

Adoption expenses (including agency fees, attorney fees, court costs, and related travel), may be eligible for a tax credit, but there is a limit to the amount of qualified expense allowed and the credit is phased out when your modified AGI reaches $199,450. (See Introduction for an explanation of modified adjusted gross income) The adoption of a child with special needs is eligible for the full annual tax credit allowed regardless of the amount of related expenses. The excess credit can be carried forward for the next five years. The cost of adoption of a spouse's child, surrogate parenting arrangements, expenses in violation of the law, or expenses paid using funds received from a government program are not eligible for this credit. Adoption payments or reimbursements from your employer are excluded from taxable income if eligibility conditions are met.

ADULT CHILDREN *See Dependents*

If you provide more than half of the support for your adult child up to age 24, you may be entitled to a tax reduction in the form of a dependent exemption. In order to be eligible, your child must be a full-time student for at least five months of the tax year or be permanently and totally disabled at any time during the year, and have income that does not exceed current limitations.

ADVERTISING EXPENSE

Advertising costs associated with a job search in your current field are tax deductible. Recent college graduates with no previous experience or internships in the prospective field are not eligible for these deductions. Advertising costs are categorized as a miscellaneous expense, subject to the 2% AGI threshold.

Advertising costs associated with business activity or revenue-producing hobbies are tax deductible. Advertising in events programs or newsletters associated with

ADVERTISING EXPENSE cont'd

political organizations or candidates is not tax deductible. Job-related advertising costs are categorized as a miscellaneous expense, subject to the 2% AGI threshold. For self-employed individuals, advertising costs associated with your business are treated as a business expense deducted directly from self-employment income.

AGI *See Adjusted Gross Income*

AIR CONDITIONING *See Home Improvements*

The cost to install or repair an air conditioner can be deducted as a medical expense if it is medically-necessary to prevent or relieve allergies or other breathing difficulties, or is doctor-prescribed for another specific condition. A home cooling system that has not been doctor-prescribed is not deductible from current income but can result in a tax reduction when you sell your home by adding to its cost basis. If you maintain a qualified home office, a portion of the cost or depreciation of your home air conditioner can be allocated to the home office.

AIR PURIFIER *See Home Improvements/Home Office*

The cost to install or repair an air purifier, humidifier, or dehumidifier can be deducted as a medical expense if it is medically-necessary to prevent or relieve allergies or other breathing difficulties, or is doctor-prescribed for another specific condition. An air purifying system that has not been doctor-prescribed is not deductible from current income but can result in a tax reduction when you sell your home by adding to its cost basis. An air purification system used in a qualified home office is tax deductible, subject to the 2% AGI threshold for miscellaneous expenses. Self-employed individuals can deduct this expense directly from self-employment income.

AIRLINE CLUBS

Membership fees for airline benefits clubs are not tax deductible even if the services and facilities are used in business travel.

ALCOHOLISM TREATMENT *See Medical Expense*

The cost of alcoholism treatment at a residential facility or as an inpatient at a hospital is tax deductible if your medical expenditures have reached the required threshold of 7.5% of your AGI. The cost of transportation to and from local AA meetings can be included in this deduction if attendance is doctor-recommended.

ALIMONY

Alimony, spousal support, and spousal maintenance are tax deductible as adjustments to gross income. To qualify for this deduction, the payments must be legally required, they must be cash payments, including checks and money orders, and the separated spouses must live apart. There is no dollar limit on this deduction.

ALTERATIONS

Expenses incurred to alter, repair, or maintain uniforms and other qualified work-related clothing are tax deductible. If job-related, alterations and other similar costs are categorized as a miscellaneous expense, subject to the 2% AGI threshold. Self-employed individuals can deduct this directly from self-employment income.

ANSWERING MACHINE & VOICE MAIL SERVICE

The cost of an answering machine or voice mail service may be tax deductible. To qualify for this deduction, the system must be essential to your work and not be reimbursed by an employer. For employees, this is a miscellaneous expense, subject to the 2% AGI threshold. Self-employed individuals can deduct this expense directly from self-employment income.

APPRAISAL FEES

Appraisal fees paid to determine the value of property to be donated to a qualified charity are tax deductible. Appraisal fees paid to determine the value of property involved in a casualty loss can also be deducted. Fees paid as part of a property settlement stemming from divorce proceedings are not deductible.

ARTWORK *See Home Office*

If you maintain a qualified home office, the cost of artwork to furnish and decorate it is tax deductible, subject to the conditions and limitations of the home office deduction. This is generally a miscellaneous expense, subject to the 2% AGI threshold. Self-employed individuals can deduct this expense directly from self-employment income.

ASSESSMENTS

Local government assessments to construct or repair sidewalks, sewers, streets, or other facilities are not tax deductible.

ATM CHARGES

Usage charges at automated tellers for accessing personal accounts are not tax deductible. Charges associated with business banking can be deducted.

"A taxpayer is someone who works for the federal government but who doesn't have to take a civil service examination."

- Ronald Reagan

ATTORNEY FEES

Attorney fees are tax deductible when they are for assistance or representation in the production or collection of taxable income including receipt of alimony, tax audits, estate planning relating to tax matters, royalties, commissions, and Social Security disputes. Attorney fees are also deductible when related to a qualified adoption or to authorize treatment for a mental illness. The criteria and limitations applied to deductible attorney fees vary by expense category.

Attorney fees are not deductible when they are for assistance or representation in personal matters, even if the outcome might be the loss of income-producing property. Nondeductible personal attorney fees include those for child custody disputes, breach of promise, preparation of a title or a will, civil or criminal charges stemming from a personal relationship, and property settlements in a divorce.

While the attorney fees associated with the collection of taxable income stemming from personal injury suits are tax deductible, those associated with determining damage awards for physical injuries can not be deducted.

AUTOMOBILE EXPENSE

If you own your car and use it exclusively in your job or business, then the entire cost of operating it can be deducted from taxable income.

The deduction can be based on either miles driven or the actual cost of maintaining and operating the car, including registration and licensing fees, insurance, gas, maintenance and repairs, tires, garage rental, parking fees, tolls, and depreciation.

All expenses must be substantiated through receipts and a mileage log.

The deduction for the business use of your personal car depends on whether you are an employee or are self-employed. As an employee, you may claim the deduction as an unreimbursed employee expense, subject to the 2% AGI threshold for miscellaneous expenses.

If you are self-employed, the cost relating to the business use of your personal car may be deducted from self-employment income as a business expense. If the car is not exclusively used for business purposes, the deductible amount is prorated to reflect this. The job-related use of your personal car can be deducted directly from self-employment income.

Automobile expenses associated with medical travel, charitable travel, job search, and other tax deductible activities may also be deducted, subject to the limitations of the associated deduction category.

AUTOMOBILE LEASE *See Automobile Expense*

The cost to lease a car used in tax deductible activities (e.g., travel related to work, charitable activities, medical treatment, or a job search) may be partly or wholly tax deductible. There are restrictions on the cost calculations for the lease, and limits on the amount of depreciation that can be deducted. All expenses must be substantiated through receipts and a mileage log.

AUTOMOBILE REGISTRATION *See Automobile Expense*

If your state calculates its automobile registration as an annual fee based on your car's value, the registration fee for your personal car is wholly deductible.

If your state bases its automobile registration fees on factors such as weight, model, vehicle age, and engine size, the fee is tax deductible if your personal car is used in tax deductible activities (e.g., travel that is related to work, charitable activities, medical treatment, or a job search). The deduction is prorated to reflect the non-personal use, and is subject to the limitations and expense threshold of the applicable deduction category.

APRIL 15 (TAX DAY)

Falls in the middle of the month that begins with 'April Fools' and ends with cries of 'May Day'.

B

BABYSITTER *See Childcare*

The cost to employ a babysitter can be tax deductible in the form of a tax credit. The babysitter must be necessary for you to earn income, the payments must be documented, and the credit may be subject to income limitations. Babysitting fees paid to you, your spouse, your children up to age 19, or another dependent can not be claimed for this deduction. However, even if a grandparent or other relative lives in the same home, you can still deduct the cost of an unrelated babysitter.

BACK SUPPORT *See Medical Expense*

A doctor-prescribed back support or pillow may be tax deductible if your medical expenses have reached the required threshold of 7.5% of your AGI.

BAD DEBTS

The unpaid balance from a personal loan may be deducted. To qualify for the deduction, it must truly be uncollectible, can not be construed as a gift, and must not violate state usury laws. Unpaid wages, back rents, and child support do not qualify for this deduction.

BANKING FEES

Banking fees assessed as service charges on personal bank accounts are not tax deductible. Certain fees charged for late payments on loans can be deducted. If the late fee is assessed as additional interest due on an outstanding balance, and the interest charges normally associated with the loan meet the criteria of tax deductibility, then the late fee is also deductible.

BAR SUPPLIES *See Office Supplies*

Bar supplies used in a qualified home office are tax deductible. If the items have a useful life of more than one year (such as refrigerators and glassware), they are treated as equipment and may be depreciated or deducted in the year of purchase based on cost and business use. Your income level may limit the deduction. For employees, this is a miscellaneous expense, subject to the 2% AGI threshold. Self-employed individuals can deduct this expense directly from self-employment income.

BARTER

Business-related goods and services that you receive through a trade or barter arrangement are reportable as income. The fair market value of goods and service you provide as barter are deductible. The criteria and limitations of the deduction will vary by the type of expense.

BATTERIES *See Office Supplies*

Batteries and other supplies used in work-related equipment and appliances or used in a qualified home office are tax deductible as a miscellaneous expense, subject to the 2% AGI threshold. Self-employed individuals can deduct this expense directly from self-employment income.

BELOW-MARKET LOANS

If you lend money to a friend at no interest or at highly favorable interest rates, you may be entitled to claim a deduction for the interest that could have been charged. The deduction is subject to conditions based on loan amount, interest charged, loan duration, use of the loan proceeds, and investment interest expense limitations. The loan should be substantiated with an enforceable note documenting the loan amount, payment terms, interest rate, and collateral offered. The interest is not deductible if the loan is used to pay personal expenses.

BEVERAGES *See Office Supplies*

The cost of supplying beverages to a home office may be tax deductible as office supplies if the beverages are helpful to the functioning of the office, and the expense is not extravagant. These costs are treated as a miscellaneous expense and may be deducted if your miscellaneous expenditures have reached the required threshold of 2% of your AGI. Self-employed individuals can deduct this expense directly from self-employment income.

BIRTH CONTROL *See Medical Expense*

Doctor-prescribed birth control may be tax deductible if your medical expenses have reached the required threshold of 7.5% of your AGI.

BLOOD SUGAR TEST KIT *See Medical Expense*

Doctor-prescribed blood sugar testing kits and supplies may be tax deductible if your medical expenses have reached the required threshold of 7.5% of your AGI.

BOATS & RVs

Boats and recreational vehicles may be treated as primary residences or vacation homes for tax purposes. A taxpayer living in a boat or RV is entitled to all home owner tax deductions, including mortgage interest deductions, capital improvement interest deductions, and property tax deductions. To qualify as a residence, the vehicle must contain cooking, sleeping, and bathroom facilities. The cost to purchase and maintain boats and recreational vehicles used for entertainment or recreation may not be deducted even if the activities serve a business purpose.

BONDS

A tax deduction can be taken for bonds and other securities that lose some or all of their value. The loss can be claimed when the security is sold, or when it is determined to be worthless. The deduction is usually limited to the original purchase price of the bond.

BOOKS & MAGAZINES & TAPES

Books, magazines, and tapes are tax deductible if they are related to work, a revenue-producing hobby, personal investments, or a job search. Books and magazines purchased for use in a qualified, tax deductible, educational activity can also be deducted. Job-related publications are a miscellaneous expense, subject to the 2% AGI threshold. Self-employed individuals can deduct this expense directly from self-employment income.

BOTTLED WATER *See Medical Expense/Office Supplies*

Doctor-prescribed bottled water may be tax deductible if your medical expenses have reached the required threshold of 7.5% of your AGI. Bottled water is not deductible if it is purchased solely to avoid additives to public water. Bottled water, water coolers, and other beverages supplied to a home office are treated as tax deductible office supplies if the beverages are helpful to the functioning of the office and the expense is not extravagant.

"I hold in my hand 1,379 pages of tax simplification."

- Congressman Delbert Latta

BREAST IMPLANTS *See Medical Expense*

Cosmetic surgery necessary to correct a deformity resulting from birth, an injury caused by an accident or trauma, or a disfiguring disease is a tax deductible expense if it meets the criteria of a qualified medical expense. Qualified medical expenses are tax deductible after reaching the required threshold of 7.5% of your AGI. Breast enhancements are not generally deductible, although exotic dancers have occasionally received Tax Court rulings permitting the deduction as a business expense.

BRIEFCASE

The cost of a briefcase or portfolio used to carry your business papers is tax deductible. For employees, it is a miscellaneous expense subject to the 2% AGI threshold. Self-employed individuals can deduct this expense directly from self-employment income.

BURIAL FEES *See Funeral Costs*

BUS FARE (JOB-RELATED) *See Business Travel*

Bus fare related to a job search, an income-producing activity, or your job may be tax deductible as qualified business travel. Regular bus travel to and from work is not deductible unless the home is a qualified business location or the travel is between work sites.

BUS FARE (MEDICAL EXPENSE)

Bus fare is deductible as a medical expense if you are traveling for a doctor's appointment or medical treatment, to obtain prescription drugs, to attend AA meetings, or to attend a medical conference on a relevant illness or condition. Qualified medical expenses are tax deductible after reaching the required threshold of 7.5% of your AGI.

BUSINESS CARDS

Business cards may be a tax deductible miscellaneous expense, subject to the 2% AGI threshold, if related to a job search, an income-producing activity such as investments or hobbies, or are an unreimbursed employee expense. Self-employed individuals can deduct this expense directly from self-employment income.

BUSINESS CONFERENCES AND CONVENTIONS *See Business Travel*

The cost of attending a convention or trade show may be tax deductible if you can document its benefit to your trade or business. The deduction includes attendance fees, travel, lodging, and 50% of meal costs. If the event is held outside of North America, you must demonstrate the reasonableness of both the event's location and your attendance in order for it to be tax deductible. Conventions held on cruise ships are subject to further limitations and restrictions, with more extensive documentation requirements. Job-related travel not reimbursed by your employer is deductible as a miscellaneous expense, subject to the 2% AGI threshold. Business travel is wholly deductible from self-employment income for self-employed individuals. Conference and convention travel that benefits your volunteer service or other charitable activities is deductible as a charitable donation, subject to the limitations of that category of deductions.

"The income tax has made more liars out of the American people than golf has."

- Will Rogers

BUSINESS PORTION OF THE HOME

If you have an area of your home used regularly and exclusively for business purposes, a portion of your home's expenses can be tax deductible as a home office expense, including utilities, real estate taxes, and mortgage interest. Non-office spaces of your home that are eligible for the home office deduction including studios, barns, garages, greenhouses, meeting rooms, and storage areas.

Separate structures on your property may qualify for this deduction. If your home office is a requirement of employment (e.g., telecommuting) or a convenience to your employer, it is tax deductible as an unreimbursed employee expense, subject to the 2% AGI threshold for miscellaneous expenses. Self-employed individuals can deduct home office expenses directly from self-employment income.

7,000,000

The number of dependents dropped from tax rolls following the Tax Reform Act of 1986 requiring individuals filing a tax return due after December 31, 1987, to include the taxpayer identification number (usually the Social Security Number) of each dependent age 5 or older.

BUSINESS TRAVEL

Business travel not fully or partially reimbursed by your employer is tax deductible as a miscellaneous expense, subject to the 2% AGI threshold. Business travel is wholly deductible for self-employed individuals. The business travel deduction includes the cost of all transportation between your home and your business destination, as well as local transportation once your destination is reached. If you use your personal car for business travel, toll charges and parking fees are included in the travel deduction, as well as the cost to operate and maintain the car, based on your automobile deduction method. Your meals as well as those for business-related entertaining are deductible when traveling away from home. You can use your actual dining costs or base the deduction on the IRS standard meal allowance established for your destination. In either case, the deduction is limited to 50% of the cost, and documentation and substantiation are required. The tax deduction for business travel may be limited by the regularity and duration of the travel.

If you remain on site for the duration of your workweek, returning home on weekends, your travel to and from the work location and your weekday living expenses may not be tax deductible. It can be determined that you and your spouse have different tax homes for travel purposes, even though you maintain a single primary residence together. If a business trip is extended an extra day to take advantage of reduced airfare, the cost of the extra meals and lodging is also tax deductible, after applying the 50% limit to meal costs. Travel that directly benefits your volunteer service or other charitable activities is deductible as a charitable contribution, subject to the limitations of that category of deductions.

C

CAB FARE (JOB-RELATED) *See Business Travel*

Cab fare related to a job search, an income-producing activity, or your job may be deductible as qualified business travel. Regular cab fare to and from work is not deductible unless the home is a qualified business location, or the travel is between work sites. Business travel that is not fully or partially reimbursed by your employer is tax deductible as a miscellaneous expense, subject to the 2% AGI threshold. Self-employed individuals can deduct this expense directly from self-employment income.

Travel that directly benefits your volunteer service or other charitable activities is deductible as a charitable contribution, subject to the limitations of that category of deductions.

CALENDARS *See Office Supplies*

Calendars and other supplies used in a qualified home office are tax deductible, subject to the 2% AGI threshold for miscellaneous expenses. Self-employed individuals can deduct this expense directly from self-employment income.

CAMPAIGN CONTRIBUTIONS

You can not deduct contributions to a political candidate, a political campaign, or a political party.

CANDY & CANDY DISPENSER

The cost of supplying candy and other snack foods to a home office is a tax deductible expense if the items are helpful to the functioning of the office, and the expense is not extravagant.

CAPITAL IMPROVEMENTS

Capital improvements to your home are not deductible from current income but can result in a tax reduction when you sell your home because you can add the cost of the improvements to the home's cost basis. Capital improvements include adding or expanding a deck, garage, room, or porch; heating, cooling, and security systems; upgrading or updating wiring, plumbing, your kitchen or bathroom, paving, or masonry; a new roof, windows, or doors; and new fixtures, built-in appliances, and systems. If you make capital improvements to your home after establishing your home office, you can allocate the business percentage of the capital expenditure to the home office. The amount is depreciated over 39 years. Improvements made to accommodate a medical need may be deductible in the current tax year.

CAPITAL LOSS

Tax deductible capital losses are losses that arise from the sale of stocks, collectibles, real estate, or other assets. Individual capital losses are tax deductible in full to the extent that they offset that year's capital gains. If your losses exceed your gains, a portion of the excess loss up to $3,000 may be used to offset ordinary income. The balance is carried forward indefinitely as an offset to future capital gains and ordinary income, subject to the same $3,000 cap per tax year.

CAR ACCIDENT/THEFT *See Casualty Loss*

A loss due to a stolen or damaged personal car is tax deductible if not reimbursed by insurance or relief agencies. The first $100 of the net loss is nondeductible. The balance of the loss in excess of 10% of your adjusted gross income (AGI) may be deducted. The undepreciated portion of a stolen or damaged business car, less insurance or relief agency proceeds, is fully deductible for self-employed individuals.

CAR DONATION *See Charitable Contributions*

When donating a car to a qualified charity, the tax deduction amount is based on either the actual resale by the charity or the value of its use by the charitable organization, not the fair market value. For most charitable donations, the maximum you can deduct in one tax year is limited to 50% of your AGI. In the event of larger donations, the portion of the deduction in excess of the cap can be carried forward to offset income in the following tax year.

CAREER COUNSELOR

Career counseling is a tax deductible miscellaneous expense, subject to the 2% AGI threshold, if it assists in improving current work status. It is not deductible if you are seeking your first job in your field or returning to a line of work in which you have you have not recently been employed.

CARPET CLEANING *See Home Office*

Cleaning costs including supplies and a cleaning service used in a qualified home office are tax deductible, subject to the 2% AGI threshold for miscellaneous expenses. Self-employed individuals can deduct this expense directly from self-employment income.

CASH DONATIONS *See Charitable Contributions*

Cash donations to charitable organizations are tax deductible. Small cash donations (to church collection plates or holiday bell-ringers, for example) do not require a receipt but must be documented in your records.

CASUALTY LOSS

A casualty loss to personal property, such as your home or car, is partially or wholly tax deductible if not covered by insurance or other disaster relief. If there is insurance or relief agency reimbursement, the unreimbursed balance of the loss can still be deducted. The loss is first reduced by applicable proceeds from insurance or relief agencies. The first $100 of the net loss is nondeductible. The balance of the loss in excess of 10% of your adjusted gross income (AGI) may be deducted. If the damage is to property used for both business and personal purposes, a portion of the loss can be allocated to the home office based on the percentage of your home used for business.

The loss can be due to theft, accident, or a casualty event such as a flood or hurricane. The loss can not be the result of neglect or willful misconduct on your part, such as failing to winterize your car or driving under the influence of drugs or alcohol. Stolen or damaged inventory is not treated as a casualty loss.

The normal $100 per incident floor for personal casualty and theft losses and the separate 10% of AGI floor are both waived for casualty and theft losses caused by Hurricane Katrina on or after 8/25/05 in the Hurricane Katrina disaster area.

CELLULAR PHONE *See Equipment/Telephone*

Cellular phone costs may be tax deductible if they are related to a job search or an income-producing activity such as investments or hobbies. Job-related cellular phone expenditures may also be deducted if not reimbursed by your employer. Cell phones are considered to have a useful life of more than one year, and are treated as equipment for tax purposes.

CHARITABLE CONTRIBUTIONS

Charitable contributions are tax deductible if made by an individual or corporation to an IRS-approved, tax-exempt nonprofit organization. Other partnerships, sole proprietorships, and limited liability corporations are not eligible for this deduction. Recipients can include charitable or religious entities, fraternal lodges, and veterans organizations.

Large donations require documentation from the receiving organization. Small donations, including holiday toys or canned goods placed in a collection bin, do not require a receipt but must be documented in your records. If you receive a book, CD, meal, or other thank you gift for your contribution, your deduction is limited to the portion of the contribution in excess of the value of the gift. A contribution of fully-depreciated assets is not tax deductible. Individuals can not claim a deduction for the value of time and services that they contribute, but the direct costs associated with volunteer service can be deducted.

For most charitable donations from an individual taxpayer, the maximum you can deduct in one tax year is limited to 50% of your AGI. In the event of larger donations, the portion of the deduction in excess of the cap can be carried forward to offset income in the following tax year.

CHARITABLE TRAVEL

Out-of-pocket travel costs incurred through charitable pursuits are tax deductible. You can deduct out-of-pocket car expenses such as gas and oil or the mileage rate if you use your car for charitable purposes. Other travel expenses, such as meals and lodging, may be deductible for overnight trips. To qualify for this deduction, there can not be a significant element of recreation involved in the charitable activities. For most charitable donations, the maximum you can deduct in one tax year is limited to 50% of your AGI.

CHAUFFEUR

The cost of your driver or chauffeur for business-related travel is a tax deductible business expense, if not reimbursed by your employer. This cost is treated as a miscellaneous expense, subject to the 2% AGI threshold. Self-employed individuals can deduct this expense directly from self-employment income.

CHILD SUPPORT

Child support payments are not tax deductible, although the payer might be entitled to claim a dependent exemption. The recipient of child support (the child or the parent who receives payment on behalf of the child) is not taxed on the resulting income.

CHILDBIRTH CLASSES *See Medical Expense*

Childbirth classes may be tax deductible if your medical expenses have reached the required threshold of 7.5% of your AGI.

CHILDCARE

The cost of qualified childcare that enables you to work may be eligible for a tax credit if documentation requirements are met. If you are married, you and your spouse must be employed part- or full-time, unless one or both partners is incapacitated or a full-time student.

Qualifying expenses may include babysitting, daycare, day camp, housekeeper/nanny/au pair, private school, and some transportation.

Childcare payments made to you, your spouse, your children up to age 19, or another dependent can not be claimed for this deduction. However, even if a grandparent, adult child, or other relative lives in your home as your dependent and is available to provide childcare, you are not obligated to employ that person; you can still pay an unrelated babysitter or daycare provider to care for your child.

Sleep-away camp and private school tuition beyond kindergarten are not eligible for this deduction.

CHILDREN AS EMPLOYEES

You may hire your children to work for your unincorporated business and pay them reasonable wages and deduct those wages from your income. If they are under the age of 18, you don't have to deduct their Social Security or Medicare tax nor do you generally have to pay state unemployment or disability taxes. The age at which a child can work depends on your state's labor laws.

CHIROPODIST/PODIATRIST *See Medical Expense*

Chiropody/podiatric treatment may be tax deductible if your medical expenses have reached the required threshold of 7.5% of your AGI.

CHIROPRACTOR *See Medical Expense*

Chiropractic treatment may be tax deductible if your medical expenses have reached the required threshold of 7.5% of your AGI.

CHRISTIAN SCIENCE PRACTITIONER *See Medical Expense*

Treatments received from a Christian Science practitioner may be tax deductible if your medical expenses have reached the required threshold of 7.5% of your AGI.

CHURCH MEMBERSHIP *See Charitable Contributions*

Membership dues paid to a church, synagogue, mosque, temple, or other religious congregation are tax deductible. The deduction must be reduced by the value of any benefits received, and the maximum you can deduct in one tax year is limited to 50% of your AGI.

CLARINET LESSONS *See Medical Expense*

Clarinet lessons, when doctor-prescribed to treat tooth misalignment, may be tax deductible if your medical expenses have reached the required threshold of 7.5% of your AGI.

"Don't tax you, don't tax me, tax that fellow behind the tree."

- Senator Russell B Long

CLEANING EXPENSE *See Home Office*

Cleaning costs, including supplies and a cleaning service, used in a qualified home office are a tax deductible miscellaneous expense, subject to the 2% AGI threshold. Self-employed individuals can deduct this expense directly from self-employment income.

CLOSING COSTS

Closing costs, points, and other charges incurred to obtain a home mortgage may be tax deductible as mortgage interest, if certain conditions are met. To qualify for this deduction, the points must be computed as a percentage of the loan, your main home must secure the loan, the funds must be used to purchase or build that home, and the points can not be paid with proceeds of the loan. Costs that do not meet these conditions may be partially deductible over the life of the loan.

CLOTHING & UNIFORMS

Work-related clothing and uniform costs may be tax deductible. In order to qualify for this deduction, the clothing must be required for your job and not be adaptable for everyday wear. Uniforms or articles of clothing that display an employer's logo or advertising may be deductible. The unreimbursed cost of purchasing, cleaning, and maintaining Job-related clothing and uniforms may be deducted as a miscellaneous expense, subject to the 2% AGI threshold. Self-employed individuals can deduct this expense directly from self-employment income.

CLOTHING DONATIONS *See Charitable Contributions*

The value of used clothing donated to a qualified charity is tax deductible, subject to the limitations of charitable donations. You may not claim the deduction for items donated directly to an individual.

CLUB MEMBERSHIP

The cost of membership in a professional association, community booster club, or chamber of commerce is tax deductible if it is necessary or beneficial to your work. The cost of membership in a country club or other facility organized for social or recreational purposes is not tax deductible. Dues paid to airline or hotel clubs are not tax deductible even if the associated travel is job-related.

COFFEE *See Office Supplies*

Supplies used in a qualified home office are tax deductible. This includes coffee and other beverage service items, as long as they are not lavish or extravagant for the circumstances, subject to the 2% AGI threshold for miscellaneous expenses. Self-employed individuals can deduct this expense directly from self-employment income.

COMMUTING

A daily commute from home to work is not tax deductible unless your home office is a qualified business location. A daily commute between work sites is a tax deductible miscellaneous expense, subject to the 2% AGI threshold, if not reimbursed by your employer. Self-employed individuals can deduct this expense directly from self-employment income.

COMPUTER *See Equipment*

The cost of a home computer used to monitor investments may be tax deductible. Its whole or primary purpose must be investment-related, and the deduction

COMPUTER cont'd

is based on the percentage of its use that is for business purposes.

The deduction includes depreciation, maintenance, repairs, supplies, and online services. A computer located in a qualified home office is also deductible. Computers and accessories are considered to have a useful life of more than one year, and are treated as equipment for tax purposes. Generally, job-related computer costs will be treated as a miscellaneous expense, subject to the 2% AGI threshold. Self-employed individuals can deduct the expense of maintaining, operating, and depreciating a computer directly from self-employment income.

CONDOMINIUM

If you maintain a qualified home office in a condominium, you can deduct a percentage of your lease and related condominium fees. If you own the condominium, you can claim an allocated percentage of its depreciation.

CONFERENCES/CONVENTIONS *See Business Travel*

CONSERVATION

The value of real estate donated for land conservation is tax deductible. If it is a partial donation in which you donate the land but retain certain rights to the property (such as an easement, mineral rights, or a remainder interest that is granted upon your death), the value of the donated portion is tax deductible.

CONTACT LENSES *See Medical Expense*

Contact lenses, including maintenance equipment, supplies, and replacement insurance premiums may be tax deductible if your medical expenses have reached the required threshold of 7.5% of your AGI.

CONTINUING EDUCATION *See Education*

Qualified job-related education expenses are tax deductible. To qualify for the deduction, the course can not lead to a new line of work, but must maintain or enhance the skills required by your current position. Job-related education required by law or your employer is also deductible. Job-related continuing education costs are subject to the 2% AGI threshold for miscellaneous expense deductions. Self-employed individuals can deduct this expense directly from self-employment income.

COOPERATIVE HOUSING

A resident of a housing co-op is entitled to two levels of deductions. The mortgage interest expense and taxes corresponding to the directly held portion of the co-op are tax deductible, as are the mortgage interest and taxes corresponding to a share of common areas. The business percentage of both levels of the deduction can be allocated to a qualified home office.

COSMETIC SURGERY *See Medical Expense*

Cosmetic surgery necessary to correct a deformity resulting from birth, an injury caused by an accident or trauma, or a disfiguring disease is a tax deductible medical expense after you have reached the required medical expense threshold of 7.5% of your AGI. Some surgeries are cosmetic in nature but also alleviate medical conditions such as eyelid lifts that improve obstructed vision or nasal surgery that improves breathing. In such instances, the surgery may be tax deductible. Breast enhancements are not generally deductible although exotic dancers have occasionally received Tax Court rulings permitting the deduction as a business expense.

COUNTRY CLUB MEMBERSHIP *See Entertaining*

The cost of membership in a golf, tennis, swimming, dining, or hunting club is not tax deductible even if there is a business element involved in the membership. You may deduct the cost of entertaining business associates at the facility, if the cost meets the criteria of a qualified entertainment expense.

COUPLES COUNSELING

Couples and relationship counseling fees are not tax deductible.

COVERDELL SAVINGS ACCOUNT *See Education*

Contributions to Coverdell education savings accounts are not tax deductible. Earnings are tax deferred and subsequent distributions are tax free if used to pay qualified education expenses. Unlike most educational deductions, tax-free Coverdell proceeds can be used for education beginning with kindergarten expenses. Eligible expenses include tuition, tutoring, books, school-based extended care, supplies, transportation, uniforms, computers, peripheral software, and internet access.

COWORKER LUNCHES *See Meals*

Workday lunches with coworkers are generally considered to be a personal expenditure and are not tax deductible. If the expense is incurred in the course of unreimbursed, qualified business travel, the deduction is limited to 50% of the cost.

CREDIT CARD INTEREST

Credit card interest for personal expenditures is not tax deductible. If credit cards are used to finance tax deductible expenditures, (e.g., tuition, medical expenses), the resultant interest can be tax deductible.

CRUISE SHIP CONVENTIONS

See Business Travel

The cost of attending a business meeting on a cruise ship may be tax deductible if you can document its benefit to your trade or business. Cruise ship conventions are subject to specific limitations and restrictions, and require more extensive documentation than traditional conferences and conventions. Qualified cruise ship travel not fully or partially reimbursed by your employer is tax deductible as a miscellaneous expense, subject to the 2% AGI threshold, after applying the 50% limit to certain costs (e.g., meals and entertainment). Self-employed individuals can deduct the cost of cruise ship travel directly from self-employment income after applying the 50% limit to certain costs. Cruise ship travel that directly benefits your volunteer service or other charitable activities is deductible as a charitable contribution, subject to the limitations of that category of deductions.

CUSTODIAL FEES

Payments of custodial or trustee fees to maintain an IRA account are tax deductible. The fees can not be debited from the IRA account, but must be paid directly to the custodian or trustee in order to qualify for this deduction.

"People who complain about taxes can be divided into two classes: men and women."

- Unknown

D

DAY CAMP *See Childcare*

Amounts paid to a qualified day camp may be eligible for a tax credit if the expense is incurred to enable you to work. Eligible dependents for this deduction include young children up to the age of 13, elderly parents, and physically or mentally disabled family members. If you run your own day camp, you can not deduct the cost to provide care for your own children or dependents. Sleep-away camp fees are not eligible for this deduction.

DAYCARE *See Childcare*

The cost of qualified daycare that enables you to work or to receive medical treatment may be deductible in the form of a tax credit if documentation requirements are met.

DECORATIONS *See Home Office*

The cost of furnishing and decorating a qualified home office may be tax deductible. To qualify for this deduction, the decor must not be lavish or extravagant for the circumstances and can not be reimbursed by your employer. Furniture and other items with a useful life greater than one year must be capitalized. Generally, decorating costs, furniture and equipment depreciation for a job-related home office are treated as a miscellaneous expense, subject to the 2% AGI threshold. Self-employed individuals can deduct this expense directly from self-employment income.

DEPENDENT CARE *See Childcare*

Dependent care may be tax deductible in the form of a tax credit, subject to income limitations. The expense must be necessary to earn income, and must meet documentation requirements. Eligible dependents for this deduction may include young children, elderly parents, and physically or mentally disabled family members, and they are not limited to those for whom you claim an exemption.

DEPENDENTS

You can claim a tax deduction in the form of a dependent exemption for your children through age 18 if you provide at least half of the cost of their support.

If your child is a full-time student between ages 18 and 24 and you continue to provide more than half the cost of the child's support, you may still be able to claim your child as a dependent.

In the case of divorce or separation, the non-custodial parent can qualify for a tax deduction if the parents have lived apart for the past six months of the calendar year, and the non-custodial parent provides more than 50% of the support.

You can claim as a dependent other household members who satisfy residency requirements and income limitations if you provide more than half of the cost of their support. Extended family members do not need to live with you to be claimed as dependents if support requirements are met.

If you have a multiple support agreement, such as the shared support of elderly parents among siblings, you may qualify for this deduction even if you do not provide more than half of their support.

DEPENDENTS cont'd

In determining what percentage of support you provide a dependent, you can include the cost of food, lodging, clothing, utilities, education, and medical expenses, as well as recreational items including summer camp, dance lessons, cable television, education, and life-cycle spending on weddings and similar events.

DEPRECIATION *See Equipment Expense*

You may claim a tax deduction for the depreciation of most types of tangible property used in your work or other income-producing activities. The property must have a useful life of more than one year, and can include buildings, vehicles, furniture, and equipment. You can also depreciate certain intangible property, such as patents, copyrights, and computer software. If you make capital improvements to your home after establishing your home office, you can allocate the business percentage of the capital expenditure to the home office.

DERMATOLOGIST *See Medical Expense*

Dermatologist visits may be tax deductible if your medical expenses have reached the required threshold of 7.5% of your AGI.

DIAPER SERVICE

The expense of a diaper service is not tax deductible.

DIET *See Medical Expense*

A doctor-prescribed diet may be tax deductible if your medical expenses have reached the required threshold of 7.5% of your AGI. If the diet requires specific food items or supplements, the deduction includes the increased food costs associated with their purchase. Fees charged to attend a diet support group may also be deductible.

DINING *See Meals*

Generally, 50% of the cost of dining may be tax deductible when it is incurred as a qualified business expense. Meal costs may also be deducted when incurred through tax deductible forms of travel such as charitable, educational, business, medical, or adoption-related travel. To qualify for this deduction, the meal can not be lavish or extravagant for its circumstances. Lunches with coworkers generally do not meet the criteria of qualified expenses. Employee dining costs are treated as a miscellaneous expense, subject to the 2% AGI threshold, after applying the 50% limit to the costs. Self-employed individuals can deduct the cost of business dining directly from self-employment income, after applying the 50% limit to the costs.

DISABILITY FUND

Employee contributions to a state disability fund are tax deductible.

DISABILITY INSURANCE

Disability insurance premiums are not tax deductible for yourself or your dependents. You may be able to deduct premiums paid to cover a former spouse if they are included in alimony.

DISASTER LOSS *See Casualty Loss*

Property damage or loss due to an event within a federally designated disaster area can be claimed as a disaster loss. The deduction can be taken in the current tax year or applied to the prior year's tax return. This option is designed to provide you with an immediate cash infusion that could result from a retroactive tax refund.

DISHES *See Office Supplies*

Dishes and other kitchen supplies used in a qualified home office are tax deductible, subject to the 2% AGI threshold for miscellaneous expenses. Self-employed individuals can deduct this expense directly from self-employment income.

DISKS (CDs, DISKETTES, DVDs, ZIP DISKS) *See Office Supplies*

Disks required for a home computer used to monitor investments may be tax deductible. The cost of supplies purchased for a computer located in a qualified home office is also deductible, subject to the 2% AGI threshold for miscellaneous expenses. Self-employed individuals can deduct this expense directly from self-employment income.

DIVORCE

Alimony, spousal support, and spousal maintenance are tax deductible as adjustments to gross income. To qualify for this deduction, the payments must be legally required, they must be cash payments, including checks and money orders, and the separated spouses must live apart. There is no dollar limit on this deduction.

DOCTOR *See Medical Expense*

Doctor visits may be tax deductible if your medical expenses have reached the required threshold of 7.5% of your AGI. The visits must be for the diagnosis, treatment, or prevention of disease, and the portion of the costs already covered by insurance, an employer, or government programs is not deductible.

DOG BOARDING

The cost to board your pet while traveling may not be deducted as a job-related travel expense. The cost to board a guard dog or other service animal, such as a guide dog, may be tax deductible. The criteria and limitations applied to service dog expenses will vary by expense category.

DONATIONS *See Charitable Contributions*

DRUGS *See Medical Expense*

Drugs and medications requiring a prescription may be tax deductible if your medical expenses have reached the required threshold of 7.5% of your AGI. Insulin costs may be deducted without a prescription. Over-the-counter medications not doctor-prescribed are not tax deductible.

DRY CLEANING *See Clothing and Uniforms*

The expense of dry cleaning work-related clothing and uniforms may be tax deductible. In order to qualify for this deduction, the clothing must be required for your job and not be adaptable for everyday wear. Costumes or articles displaying an employer's logo or advertising may be deductible, subject to the 2% AGI threshold for miscellaneous expenses. Self-employed individuals can deduct this expense directly from self-employment income if it is a normal and necessary expense of the business.

DUES

Dues paid to unions or professional associations may be tax deductible as a qualified business expense if membership is necessary or beneficial to your work. The cost of dues is deductible subject to the 2% AGI threshold for miscellaneous expenses. Self-employed individuals can deduct this expense directly from self-employment income.

E

EDUCATION

Education expenses for yourself, your spouse, and your dependents may be tax deductible or provide tax benefits in the form of tax credits, subject to income restrictions, deduction limitations, and tax filing status. Education tax incentives include the Hope credit, the Lifetime Learning credit, Educational Savings Accounts (ESAs), penalty-free withdrawals from traditional and Roth IRAs, deductions of student loan interest, qualified tuition programs, educational assistance programs, and the tuition and fees deduction.

Doctor-recommended special education for a child with learning disabilities caused by mental or physical impairments may be tax deductible if your medical expenses have reached the required threshold of 7.5% of your AGI.

EDUCATION cont'd

Education expenses related to your current work may be tax deductible if your employer does not reimburse the expenses. To qualify for this deduction the course or program can not lead to a new line of work, but must maintain or enhance the skills required by your current position. .These costs are treated as a miscellaneous expense, subject to the 2% AGI threshold.

The costs associated with travel to attend a work-related class or seminar are tax deductible. To qualify for the deduction, the class can not be taken to enhance personal growth or personal investments. Unreimbursed employee educational travel costs are treated as a miscellaneous expense, subject to the 2% AGI threshold. Self-employed individuals can deduct work-related educational travel expenses directly from self-employment income. Recreational travel generally beneficial to your job is not tax deductible.

ELECTIVE DEFERRALS

Contributions to a variety of retirement savings plans are treated as deferrals to taxable income. Funds such as the 401(k), simplified employee pension (SEP), defined contribution plan, defined benefit plan, and savings incentive match plan (SIMPLE) may all qualify for this deferral. There may be a limit on the deductible portion based on the type of savings vehicle and your income.

"The trick is to stop thinking of it as 'your' money."

- anonymous auditor for the Internal Revenue Service

ELECTRIC BILL *See Home Office*

Electricity and other utility operating expenses associated with a qualified home office are tax deductible. Usage is allocated to the home office based on the percentage of the home used for business, or at a greater rate if a high level of utility usage can be attributed to the home office. Job-related home office expenses are tax deductible after reaching the required miscellaneous expense threshold of 2% of your AGI. Self-employed individuals can deduct work-related utility expenses directly from self-employment income.

EMPLOYEE EXPENSE

An expense common to your trade or business but which is not reimbursed by your employer may be tax deductible. In order to qualify, the expense must be appropriate and helpful to your work, or be required as a condition of your employment or for the convenience of your employer. This includes unreimbursed expenses for business-related travel and education, as well as the expenses associated with a home office. In most cases, the costs are deductible as a miscellaneous expense after you have met the expense threshold of 2% of your AGI.

EMPLOYMENT AGENCY FEES *See Job Search Expense*

Employment agency fees, including executive recruiter fees, incurred through a qualified job search may be tax deductible. The search must be within your present field, without a substantial break between your last employment and the job search. Qualified expenses may be deducted as a miscellaneous expense, subject to the 2% AGI threshold, even if the job search does not lead to a new job.

ENTERTAINING

Hosting business associates at recreational or entertainment events is tax deductible if it directly relates to the conducting of business, or precedes or follows a business discussion. Eligible associates include established and prospective clients, partners, and professional service providers such as bankers and accountants. The event can not be lavish and extravagant, and the deduction is limited to 50% of the expense. Job-related entertaining is treated as a miscellaneous expense, subject to the 2% AGI threshold, after applying the 50% limit to the costs. Self-employed individuals can deduct the cost of business entertaining directly from self-employment income after applying the 50% limit to the cost.

THEY SAY POLITICS MAKES STRANGE BEDFELLOWS...BUT IT'S THE TAXPAYER WHO HAS THE NIGHTMARE.

EQUIPMENT

The expense incurred to purchase equipment may be tax deductible. For tax purposes, equipment refers to property with a useful life of more than one year. This includes items for use in a home office (e.g., computers, telephones, cell phones, copiers, printers, fax machines, office furniture, software) as well as the cost of tools and equipment used in your work. The cost of the equipment may be depreciated or deducted in the year of purchase or the year placed in service. There is a limit on the dollar amount of assets that can be expensed in the first year. Your income level may limit the amount of the deduction.

Included in this deduction is equipment purchased to monitor investments, for use in a revenue-producing hobby, and for use in a qualified home office. Equipment purchased for the convenience of your employer or as a requirement of your employment is tax deductible if your employer does not reimburse the cost. Qualified job-related equipment costs and depreciation can be deducted as a miscellaneous expense, subject to the 2% AGI threshold. The cost of equipment employed in volunteer duties is treated as a charitable contribution and may be tax deductible to a maximum of 50% of your AGI.

ERISA PLAN *See Retirement Savings*

ESTATE PLANNING

The legal fees associated with estate planning tax matters are tax deductible as a miscellaneous expense subject to the 2% AGI threshold. The cost of will preparation may not be included in the deduction.

ESTIMATED TAX PENALTIES

Penalties resulting from the late payment or underpayment of estimated taxes are not deductible. Accountant fees associated with determining taxes due are a tax deductible expense.

EXCHANGE STUDENT *See Charitable Contributions*

The cost of hosting an exchange student may be tax deductible as a charitable contribution. To be eligible, the exchange program must be sponsored by a qualified charitable organization, and the expenses must be documented. College exchange programs do not qualify for this deduction.

EXECUTIVE RECRUITER FEES
See Job Search Expense

Recruiting fees incurred through a qualified job search may be tax deductible. The search must be within your present field, without a substantial break between your last employment and the job search. Qualified expenses may be deducted even if the job search does not lead to a new job.

"The hardest thing to understand in the world is the income tax."

-Albert Einstein

EXEMPTIONS

Personal tax exemptions are not true tax deductions, but they reduce your taxable income. Generally, you are allowed one tax exemption for yourself (if you are not claimed as a dependent by a parent or guardian), one tax exemption for your spouse (if you are married and filing a joint tax return), and one tax exemption for each dependent on your tax return.

To claim the exemption for a spouse, you must be married on the last tax day of the year, and your spouse can not be filing a separate return claiming his or her own exemption.

If you and your spouse file separately, you can claim the spouse's exemption only if he or she had no gross income and was not a dependent of another taxpayer.

If you are not married but live together in a common law marriage that is recognized in the state where you reside, or began the common law marriage in a state where it is recognized, then the marriage is recognized under federal law and you may file jointly and claim two personal exemptions on a joint return. You may not claim a partner as your dependent if your relationship violates local law.

A child's exemption can be claimed if he or she was born alive or adopted by you on or before December 31. This includes adult children who satisfy the income limitations and dependency criteria.

EXEMPTIONS cont'd

In the case of joint custody, generally the custodial parent is entitled to the child's exemption, unless the non-custodial parent provided more than half of the child's support. The dependency exemption can not be split between parents sharing custody. Which parent claims the exemption may be changed from year to year.

Other dependents can be claimed if they satisfy the criteria of familial or household relationship, U.S. citizenship, dependency, income limitations, and filing status. In all cases, the tax exemption is not available for individuals who are claimed as dependents on someone else's tax return.

EXERCISE EQUIPMENT *See Medical Expense*

Exercise equipment prescribed by a doctor to treat a specific medical condition may be tax deductible if your medical expenses have reached the required threshold of 7.5% of your AGI.

EXTERMINATION & PEST CONTROL

Exterminating costs including supplies and a pest control service for a qualified home office are tax deductible. If the service is performed throughout your home, a percentage of the costs reflecting the business portion of your home can be allocated to the home office. The cost of pest control is deductible, subject to the 2% AGI threshold for miscellaneous expenses. Self-employed individuals can deduct this expense directly from self-employment income.

EYEGLASSES *See Medical Expense*

Prescription eyeglasses and prescription sunglasses may be tax deductible if your medical expenses have reached the required threshold of 7.5% of your AGI.

F

FAX MACHINE *See Equipment*

FERTILITY TREATMENT *See Medical Expense*

Doctor-prescribed fertility treatments may be tax deductible if your medical expenses have reached the required threshold of 7.5% of your AGI.

FINANCIAL PLANNER

Consultation fees paid to a financial planner are tax deductible. Commissions paid to a financial planner may not be deducted.

FIREWOOD *See Home Office*

A portion of the cost of firewood used to heat your home may be allocated to the home office. It is tax deductible as a miscellaneous expense, subject to the 2% AGI threshold. Self-employed individuals can deduct this expense directly from self-employment income.

FLOWERS *See Gifts/Home Office*

Flowers and floral arrangements purchased to decorate a home office or other workspace are tax deductible. As a work-related cost it is treated as a miscellaneous expense subject to the 2% AGI threshold. Self-employed individuals can deduct the cost directly from self-employment income. Flowers purchased as gifts for coworkers, customers, clients, and other business associates can be deducted subject to the annual limit of $25 per recipient.

FOREIGN CONVENTIONS *See Business Travel*

The cost of attending a convention held outside of the United States may be tax deductible. Foreign conventions are subject to the same restrictions, limitations, and documentation requirements as those held domestically. In addition, you must demonstrate the reasonableness of the location with respect to the purpose, sponsoring organization, and attendees of the event.

FOREIGN TAXES

Taxes paid to other governments may be deductible in the form of a tax credit. Taxes imposed by governments with which the United States does not maintain diplomatic relations that have been identified as providing support to terrorists, will not result in a tax credit or deduction.

FOSTER CARE

Payments received to care for an unlimited number of foster children under the age of 19 are excluded from taxable income. In order to qualify for this exclusion, the payments must be made by a state or local agency, or a qualified, tax-exempt private placement agency. In the case of difficulty of care payments, the number of special needs children eligible for exclusions from income is limited to 10 children under the age of 19 and 5 children 19 years of age or older.

In levying taxes and in shearing sheep it is well to stop when you get down to the skin.

- Austin O'Malley
(physician/humorist)

FURNITURE *See Equipment*

The cost of furnishing and decorating a qualified home office may be tax deductible. To qualify for this deduction, the decor must not be lavish or extravagant for the circumstances and can not be reimbursed by your employer.

Furniture and other items with a useful life of more than one year can be depreciated. Generally, furniture depreciation for a job-related home office is treated as a miscellaneous expense, subject to the 2% AGI threshold. Self-employed individuals can deduct this expense directly from self-employment income.

FUNERAL COSTS

Burial, cremation, and other funeral costs are not tax deductible on an individual income tax return.

300,000

The number of trees that give their lives annually to produce the amount of paper necessary to print IRS documents.

G

GAMBLING LOSSES

Gambling losses may be tax deductible. You may not deduct more than the amount of gambling income reported on the same tax return. You must be able to document the losses through receipts, tickets, or statements. Gambling losses are NOT subject to the threshold of 2% of your AGI.

GARBAGE COLLECTION *See Home Office*

A portion of your home's services and utilities is tax deductible if they help sustain or support the functioning of a qualified home office. Usage is allocated to the home office based on the percentage of the home used for business, or at a greater rate if a high level of usage can be attributed to the functioning of the office. The cost of garbage collection is deductible, subject to the 2% AGI threshold for miscellaneous expenses. Self-employed individuals can deduct this expense directly from self-employment income.

GARDENING/LAWN CARE/LANDSCAPING

A home gardening or landscaping service is not tax deductible (unless you work in the industry and it serves to demonstrate your product line or service offerings), even if you maintain a qualified home office.

"But in this world nothing can be said to be certain, except death and taxes."

- Benjamin Franklin

GASOLINE *See Automobile Expense*

If you own or lease a car and use it in your work or other revenue-producing activities, then the cost of operating it can be deducted from taxes. The deduction can be based on either miles driven or the actual costs of maintaining and operating the car. Fuel costs are deductible if the deduction is based on actual costs, subject to the threshold of 2% of your AGI for miscellaneous expenses. Self-employed individuals can deduct this expense directly from self-employment income.

GIFTS

Gifts to individuals with whom you have past, present, or potential business relations are tax deductible. The amount of the deduction is limited to $25 per person per year, documentation of the gift expense is required, and substantiation of the business purpose must be provided. Tax deductible gift expenses can be incurred through business activities, revenue-producing hobbies, or investment activities. Non-cash gifts such as meals and entertainment may also be deductible.

GOLF

Hosting business associates at a golf course is tax deductible if it directly relates to the conducting of business, or precedes or follows a business discussion. Eligible associates include established and prospective employees, clients, agents, partners, and professional service providers such as bankers and accountants. The deduction is limited to 50% of the expense, and may not include the cost of membership at a golf club or country club. When golfing in a charity golf tournament or outing, the greens fees and value of other benefits, such as beverages and dining, must be subtracted from the event cost to determine the tax deductible portion of your contribution.

GREETING & HOLIDAY CARDS

The cost to purchase and mail greeting and holiday cards to individuals with whom you have past, present, or potential business relations is tax deductible, subject to the threshold of 2% of your AGI for miscellaneous expenses. Self-employed individuals can deduct this expense directly from self-employment income.

GUARD DOG

The costs associated with maintaining a guard dog are tax deductible. The deduction is based on usage allocated to the home office at a rate based on the business use of the home, or may be wholly deductible if the dog provides security exclusively for a separate business structure. The cost to board a guard dog or other service animal can be deducted as a job-related travel expense, subject to the 2% AGI threshold for miscellaneous expenses. The cost of the dog may be depreciated.

TAX SHELTER

A smart business practice that, absent tax considerations, is a stupid business practice.

• H •

HAIR TRANSPLANTS

Hair transplants are not a tax deductible expense.

HANDICAP ACCESSIBILITY *See Home Improvements*

HEALTH CLUB *See Medical Expense*

The cost of a health club membership for a doctor-prescribed exercise or weight loss program is tax deductible as a medical expense if it meets the criteria of a qualified medical expense. You can deduct the separate fees a health club charges for weight loss activities. Both deductions are available if your medical expenditures have reached the required threshold of 7.5% of your AGI.

HEALTH INSURANCE *See Medical Expense/Medicare*

Health insurance premiums are tax deductible. The deduction can include policies that cover prescription drugs, replacement contact lenses, long-term care, and the portion of your car insurance premiums that provides medical coverage. Medicare premiums for supplemental coverage are deductible; Part A premiums can be deducted if you enroll voluntarily and are not already covered under Social Security or if you are a governmental employee who paid Medicare tax. Qualified health insurance costs are tax deductible if you have reached the required threshold of 7.5% of your AGI. The employer-paid portion of health insurance premiums and pre-tax contributions are not deductible.

HEALTH SAVINGS ACCOUNT (HSA)

Contributions to health savings accounts (HSAs) are treated as an adjustment to gross income. Withdrawals from HSAs are tax-free if the proceeds are applied toward medical expenses. To contribute to an HSA, you must be covered by a health insurance policy with a high deductible, and you can not be covered by Medicare.

HEARING AIDS *See Medical Expense*

Doctor-prescribed hearing aids may be tax deductible if your medical expenses have reached the required threshold of 7.5% of your AGI.

HEATING DEVICE *See Home Improvements/Medical Expense*

The cost of a heating device can be deducted as a medical expense if it is doctor-prescribed to treat a specific medical condition and your medical expenditures have reached the required threshold of 7.5% of your AGI. If it is installed as a permanent fixture, the deduction is limited to the extent to which the device does not increase your home's value.

HEATING EXPENSE *See Home Office*

A portion of your home's heating expense is tax deductible if it helps sustain or support the functioning of a qualified home office. Qualified home office expenses can be deducted as a miscellaneous expense, subject to the 2% AGI threshold. Self-employed individuals can deduct this expense directly from self-employment income.

HOBBIES

The costs associated with a hobby are tax deductible to the extent that the hobby generates taxable income.

HOLIDAY TIPS/HOLIDAY GIFTS
See Gifts

Holidays tips and gifts to individuals with whom you have past, present, or potential business relations are tax deductible. The amount of the deduction is limited to $25 per person per year, documentation of the gift expense is required, and substantiation of the business purpose must be provided. Qualified gifts and tips are treated as a miscellaneous expense, subject to the 2% AGI threshold. Self-employed individuals can deduct this expense directly from self-employment income.

HOME ENTERTAINING *See Entertaining*

The cost of entertaining business associates in your home may be tax deductible, subject to limitations of deductibility. In order to qualify for the deduction, a substantial and bona fide business discussion must directly precede or follow the social engagement. The event can not be lavish and extravagant, and the deduction is generally limited to 50% of the expense. Entertaining business associates in your home is treated as a miscellaneous expense, subject to the 2% AGI threshold after applying the applicable 50% limit to the costs. Self-employed individuals can deduct the cost of business entertaining directly from self-employment income after applying the applicable 50% limit to the cost.

HOME EQUITY LOAN

The interest paid on home equity loans for up to two residences may be deducted from taxable income. To qualify for this deduction, the debt must be secured by your home(s), the loans can not total more than $1,000,000, and the money must have been borrowed to buy, build, or improve your primary and/or second home (home acquisition debt).

HOME EQUITY LOAN cont'd

Additionally, the interest on home equity loans that do not qualify as home acquisition debt can be deducted up to a loan amount of $100,000, subject to the $1,000,000 limit of the total debt.

HOME GYM *See Medical Expense*

The cost of home gym or exercise equipment for a doctor-prescribed exercise or weight loss program to treat a specific condition may be tax deductible if your medical expenses have reached the required threshold of 7.5% of your AGI.

HOME HEALTH CARE *See Medical Expense*

Home health care costs may be tax deductible if your medical expenses have reached the required threshold of 7.5% of your AGI. Eligible dependents for this deduction include children, elderly parents, and physically or mentally disabled family members.

"There's nothing wrong with teenagers that becoming taxpayers won't cure."

- anonymous

HOME IMPROVEMENTS

The cost of medically-necessary home improvements may be tax deductible as medical expenses to the extent to which the improvements do not increase your home's value. The costs must not be lavish or extravagant for the circumstances, and the deduction excludes additional expenses incurred for architectural or aesthetic reasons. Medically-necessary home improvements may include entrance and exit ramps, widening doorways and hallways, modified hardware, railings and hand grips, and similar modifications. Qualified medical expenses are tax deductible after reaching the required threshold of 7.5% of your AGI.

Home improvements classified as capital improvements can result in a tax reduction when you sell your home because their expense adds to its cost basis. Capital improvements to your home can include adding or expanding a deck, garage, room, or porch; heating, cooling, and security systems; upgrading or updating wiring, plumbing, renovating a kitchen or bathroom, paving, or masonry; a new roof, windows, or doors; and new fixtures, built-in appliances, and systems. If you make capital improvements to your home after establishing your home office, you can allocate the business percentage used for the home office.

HOME OFFICE

The cost of operating an office from your home may be tax deductible. To qualify for a home office tax deduction, you must demonstrate that the designated space is exclusively and regularly a place of business. Non-office spaces of your home that are eligible for the home office deduction include studios, barns, garages, greenhouses, meeting rooms, and storage areas. Separate structures on your property may qualify for this deduction.

If the office is within your house, the household expenses that indirectly relate to the home office (such as taxes, utilities, and maintenance projects) can be apportioned to the space, along with the direct expenses of the home office (such as office supplies, equipment, and furnishings). The allocation is based on either the number of rooms used or the square footage dedicated to the home office.

Deductible expenses include a portion of the home mortgage interest or rent, utilities, property taxes, insurance, repairs, and maintenance costs. The home office deduction is limited by the amount of net business income generated from the home office activity.

Deductions in excess of the net business income can not be deducted from other forms of income, although they may be carried over to the next tax year. Self-employed individuals can deduct this expense directly from self-employment income.

HOME OWNER ASSOCIATION FEE

Home owner association fees are not tax deductible unless you are eligible for the home office deduction, in which case a portion of your home owner association fees may be deducted as a home office expense, subject to the 2% AGI threshold for miscellaneous expenses.

HOME SCHOOLING

If you home school your children, you can not deduct the cost of classroom materials and other related expenses from your federal taxes. Some states provide education credits and deductions to home school families on their state income tax returns.

HOSIERY *See Medical Expense*

Doctor-prescribed hosiery that alleviates, for example, circulatory conditions, may be tax deductible if your medical expenses have reached the required threshold of 7.5% of your AGI.

HOUSE PAINTING

The cost of painting your home is not generally tax deductible. If you maintain a home office within your house, a portion of the painting costs can be allocated to the home office and may be tax deductible, subject to the 2% AGI threshold for miscellaneous expenses. Self-employed individuals can deduct this expense directly from self-employment income. The cost of paint removal is treated as a tax deductible medical expense if the paint is lead-based and a family member or dependent suffers from lead poisoning, subject to the 7.5% AGI threshold for medical expenses.

I

IMMIGRATION VISA

Expenses associated with immigration such as obtaining an H-1B visa or green card are not tax deductible.

IN VITRO FERTILIZATION *See Medical Expense*

Doctor-prescribed in vitro fertilization procedures and treatments may be tax deductible if your medical expenses have reached the required threshold of 7.5% of your AGI.

INCENTIVES, PRIZES, & AWARDS

The cost of providing sales incentives, prizes and awards for employees, coworkers, customers, vendors, and other business associates is tax deductible, subject to the 2% AGI threshold if not reimbursed by your employer, or wholly deductible from self-employment income if you are self-employed.

INCOME TAX

State, city, and county income taxes are tax deductible on your federal tax return. You may elect to deduct state and local general sales tax in place of the income tax deduction. This option is available for all filers, but is especially recommended for residents of states without income taxes. You may deduct actual sales tax paid or an estimate based on the IRS optional sales tax tables.

INHERITANCE

Most property received through an inheritance is not subject to federal inheritance tax. While some inherited income is taxable, the amount of property and assets excluded from federal taxes is large enough to allow most gifts, cash, below-market sales, and forgiven debts to avoid federal income taxes. Many states impose estate taxes with much smaller exclusions.

INSURANCE (AUTOMOBILE) *See Automobile Expense*

If you own your car and use it exclusively for business, then the entire cost of insuring it can be tax deductible. If the car is used for a combination of work-related functions and personal business, the deduction can be prorated to reflect this. You must base your automobile expense deduction on actual operating costs rather than mileage in order to deduct the insurance expense. As an employee, unreimbursed costs associated with the business use of your personal car are treated as a miscellaneous expense, subject to the 2% AGI threshold. Self-employed individuals can deduct this expense directly from self-employment income.

INSURANCE (HEALTH) *See Medical Expense*

Health insurance premiums, contact lens replacement insurance, an age-determined portion of long-term care insurance, supplemental Medicare premiums, and student health fees may be tax deductible if your medical expenses have reached the required threshold of 7.5% of your AGI. For self-employed individuals, the cost of health insurance is wholly deductible as an adjustment to gross income on page 1 of the 1040 form.

INSURANCE (LIABILITY)

General liability insurance purchased to mitigate the risk of losses from events associated with your business activity or home office is a tax deductible expense. If the cost is not reimbursed by your employer, the expense is generally subject to the 2% AGI threshold for miscellaneous expenses. Self-employed individuals can deduct this expense directly from self-employment income.

INSURANCE (LIFE)

You may not deduct the cost of life insurance premiums for yourself or your dependents. Insurance premiums included in alimony may be deducted as alimony.

INSURANCE (UNEMPLOYMENT)

Voluntary contributions to an unemployment benefit fund through a union or a privately held fund are not tax deductible. If your state requires payments to a state unemployment fund, those payments are deductible.

INTEREST EXPENSE

The interest on the first $1,000,000 borrowed to buy, build, or improve your primary and second home is deductible as home acquisition debt. Home mortgage interest for up to two residences is tax deductible.

The interest on $100,000 of home equity lines of credit that do not qualify as home acquisition debt can be deducted, subject to the $1,000,000 limit for combined debt. A portion of home mortgage interest can be allocated to a qualified home office based on the percentage of the home used for business.

The interest paid to finance investments is tax deductible, unless the investment vehicle generates tax-exempt income.

INTEREST EXPENSE cont'd

A limited portion of the interest paid on a qualified student loan is tax deductible as an adjustment to gross income.

The interest paid on car loans, credit cards, and installment purchases is not tax deductible. Interest paid on personal loans can be deducted as a business expense if the proceeds are used for business purposes.

INTERNET ACCESS *See Home Office/Telephone*

The cost of internet access for a home computer used to monitor investments is tax deductible. The cost of internet access for a computer located in a qualified home office is also tax deductible. If the costs are not reimbursed by your employer, the expense is subject to the 2% AGI threshold for miscellaneous expenses. Self-employed individuals can deduct this expense directly from self-employment income.

INVESTMENT EXPENSE

Investment newsletter subscriptions, the cost of computer and online services, fees paid to financial planners, and the rental fee on a safe deposit box to store securities are all tax deductible investment expenses. Investment-related costs are treated as a miscellaneous expense, generally subject to the 2% AGI threshold.

INVESTMENT INTEREST

Interest on money borrowed for investment purposes is tax deductible to the extent that it offsets your net investment income. Investment interest is not tax deductible if the borrowed funds are used to purchase or carry municipal bonds.

INVESTMENT LOSS *See Capital Loss*

Losses that arise from the sale of stocks, collectibles, real estate, or other assets are tax deductible in full to the extent that they offset that year's capital gains. If your losses exceed your gains, a portion of the excess loss up to $3,000 may be used to offset ordinary income. The balance is carried forward indefinitely as an offset to future capital gains and ordinary income, subject to the same $3,000 cap per tax year.

IRA *See Retirement Savings*

IRA FEES

Payments of custodial or trustee fees to maintain an IRA account are tax deductible. The fees can not be debited from the IRA account, but must be paid directly to the custodian or trustee in order to qualify for this deduction.

"The art of taxation consists in so plucking the goose as to obtain the largest amount of feathers with the least amount of hissing."

- Jean-Baptiste Colbert
(French Minister of Finance under Louis XIV)

·J·K·

JOB SEARCH EXPENSE

Expenses incurred through a job search may be tax deductible. The search must be within your present field, without a substantial break between your last employment and the job search. Qualified expenses may be deducted even if the job search does not lead to a new job. Eligible expenses include employment agency and executive recruiter fees, resume and portfolio preparation costs, career counseling, classified advertising, related travel expenses, and fees for legal counseling to protect your employment status. These costs are treated as a miscellaneous expense, subject to the 2% AGI threshold. Recent college graduates with no experience or internships in their prospective field are not eligible for these deductions.

KITCHEN SUPPLIES *See Office Supplies*

Kitchen supplies (including dishes, paper goods, and break room refreshments) used in a qualified home office are tax deductible, subject to the 2% AGI threshold for miscellaneous expenses. Self-employed individuals can deduct this expense directly from self-employment income.

KLEENEX *See Office Supplies*

L

LAPTOP COMPUTER *See Equipment*

A laptop computer used in a home office or to monitor investments may be tax deductible. Its whole or primary purpose must be job- or investment-related, and the deduction is based on the percentage used for business or investment purposes.

The deduction includes depreciation, maintenance, repairs, supplies, and online services. Computers and accessories are considered to have a useful life of more than one year, and are treated as equipment for tax purposes.

Qualified job-related equipment costs and depreciation can be deducted as a miscellaneous expense, subject to the 2% AGI threshold. Self-employed individuals can deduct this expense directly from self-employment income.

The cost of equipment employed in volunteer duties is treated as a charitable contribution and may be tax deductible to a maximum of 50% of your AGI.

LASER EYE SURGERY *See Medical Expense*

Laser eye surgery to correct a medical condition may be tax deductible if your medical expenses have reached the required threshold of 7.5% of your AGI. Laser eye surgery for strictly cosmetic reasons is not tax deductible.

LATE PAYMENT PENALTY

Late charges assessed on the repayment of personal debt such as car loans and credit card balances are not tax deductible. Late payment fees charged on loans may be deducted if the fee is assessed as additional interest due on an outstanding balance, and if the interest charges normally associated with the loan meet the criteria of tax deductibility.

LAUNDRY & DRY CLEANING *See Clothing & Uniforms*

The cost of laundering and cleaning work-related clothing and uniforms may be tax deductible. In order to qualify for this deduction, the clothing must be required for your job and not be adaptable for everyday wear, and may include uniforms or articles displaying an employer's logo or advertising. Work-related laundry and dry cleaning is subject to the 2% AGI threshold for miscellaneous expenses. Self-employed individuals can deduct this expense directly from self-employment income if it is a normal and necessary expense of the business.

LEASE *See Automobile Expense*

You may deduct the cost of leasing a car when the car is employed in tax deductible activities. This includes work-related travel, charitable activities, medical treatment, or a job search. There are restrictions on the cost calculations for the lease, and limits on the amount of depreciation that can be deducted. All expenses must be substantiated through receipts and a mileage log.

We've had the New Deal and the Fair Deal. Some taxpayers are calling what we have now the Ordeal.

LEGAL FEES *See Attorney Fees*

LICENSES

The fee for a personal driver's license is not tax deductible even if the license is required by your employer or is essential to the performance of your job's duties. The unreimbursed cost to obtain a specially endorsed license necessary to the performance of your job is tax deductible and is generally subject to the 2% AGI threshold, although self-employed individuals can deduct this expense directly from self-employment income.

Business licenses required by the city, state, or federal government are tax deductible. Self-employed individuals can deduct this expense directly from self-employment income. Fees for dog licenses, and hunting and fishing licenses are not tax deductible.

LIFE INSURANCE

You may not deduct the cost of life insurance premiums for yourself or your dependents. Life insurance premiums included in alimony payments to a former spouse can be deducted.

LINE OF CREDIT *See Home Equity Loan*

The interest paid on home equity lines of credit for up to two residences may be deducted from taxable income. The interest on the first $1,000,000 borrowed to buy, build, or improve your primary and/or second home is deductible as home acquisition debt. Additionally, the interest on $100,000 of home equity lines of credit that do not qualify as home acquisition debt can be deducted, subject to the $1,000,000 limit for combined debt.

LOANS

The interest paid to finance investments is tax deductible except when the investment generates tax-exempt income. The interest paid on student loans is an adjustment to gross income, within qualifying income limits. The interest paid on car loans, credit cards, and installment purchases is not tax deductible. Interest paid on personal loans can be deducted as a business expense if the proceeds are used for business assets or activity.

LOBBYING EXPENSE

In most cases, you can not deduct lobbying expenses incurred in order to influence legislation, influence the public on legislative matters, influence the actions of an executive branch official, or participate in the campaign of a candidate for public office. A portion of your dues or contributions to a tax-exempt organization may be nondeductible if that organization participates in lobbying activities. A limited tax deduction may be taken if lobbying expenses are an ordinary and necessary expense of carrying on your trade or business.

LONG-TERM CARE INSURANCE

An age-determined portion of the cost of long-term care insurance may be tax deductible if your medical expenses have reached the required threshold of 7.5% of your AGI. For self-employed individuals, the cost of health insurance is wholly deductible as an adjustment to gross income.

"When there is an income tax, the just man will pay more and the unjust less on the same amount of income."

- Plato

LOSS *See Casualty Loss/Capital Loss*

A loss to personal property due to an event such as fire, flood, or earthquake is tax deductible. The loss is first reduced by applicable proceeds from insurance or relief agencies. The first $100 of the net loss is nondeductible. The balance of the loss in excess of 10% of your adjusted gross income (AGI) may be deducted. If the damage is suffered by the home office or other business-related assets, self-employed individuals can deduct the net loss directly from other income on the 1040 without first reducing the loss by 10% of the AGI. If the damage is to property used for both business and personal purposes, a portion of the loss can be allocated to the home office based on the percentage of your home used for business. The loss can not be the result of neglect or willful misconduct on your part, such as failing to winterize your car or driving under the influence of drugs or alcohol.

Capital losses arise from the unsuccessful sale of stocks, collectibles, or real estate. Capital losses are tax deductible in full to the extent that they offset that year's capital gains. If your losses exceed your gains, a portion of the excess loss up to $3,000 may be used to offset ordinary income. The balance is carried forward indefinitely as an offset to future capital gains and future ordinary income, subject to the same $3,000 cap per tax year.

"Pity the poor taxpayer who has the whole government on his payroll."

- anonymous

LOST PROPERTY

You can not claim a tax deduction for mislaid property that merely disappears. In order to qualify as a casualty loss, it must disappear as the result of an event that is deemed sudden, unexpected, or unusual (e.g., a diamond ring that falls off your broken hand in a car accident). The deduction is derived by reducing the loss per casualty event by $100 and then by 10% of AGI. The loss is not tax deductible if it is the result of neglect or willful misconduct on your part.

LOTTERY TICKET *See Gambling Losses*

You may deduct the cost of losing lottery tickets to the extent that they offset gambling winnings. You may not deduct more than the amount of lottery income reported on the same tax return. You must be able to document the losses through receipts, tickets, or statements. Lottery losses are NOT subject to the threshold of 2% of your AGI.

LUNCHES *See Meals*

TAX REFORM
A deduction that benefits you.

TAX LOOPHOLE
A deduction that benefits someone else.

M

MAGAZINES

Magazines, books, and tapes are tax deductible if they are related to work, a revenue-producing hobby, personal investments, or a job search. Books and magazines purchased for use in a qualified, tax deductible, educational activity can also be deducted. The unreimbursed cost of these publications is a miscellaneous expense, subject to the 2% AGI threshold. Self-employed individuals can deduct this expense directly from self-employment income.

MAPS

The cost of maps, map books, atlases, and guidebooks used in the course of business-related travel is tax deductible. As an employee, these costs, if not reimbursed through a travel allowance, are treated as a miscellaneous expense subject to the 2% AGI threshold. Self-employed individuals can deduct this expense directly from self-employment income.

MARRIAGE LICENSE

Marriage license fees are not tax deductible.

MASSAGE *See Medical Expense*

Massages can be tax deductible if they meet the criteria of a qualified medical expense. To qualify, they must be doctor-prescribed to treat a specific medical condition, and your medical expenditures must have reached the required threshold of 7.5% of your AGI. Massages to reduce emotional stress or to enhance general well-being are not tax deductible.

MEALS

Generally, you can deduct 50% of the cost of meals when the expense is incurred through work-related activity. A portion of meal costs can also be deducted when incurred through tax deductible forms of travel such as charitable, educational, business, medical, or adoption-related travel. To qualify for this deduction, the meal can not be lavish or extravagant for its circumstances. Lunches with coworkers are usually treated as a personal expense and are not generally tax deductible unless the expense is incurred while traveling away from home on business. For qualified work-related lunches not reimbursed by your employer, costs are treated as a miscellaneous expense subject to the 2% AGI threshold, after applying the 50% limit to the costs. Self-employed individuals can deduct the cost of business dining directly from self-employment income, after applying the 50% limit to the costs.

"From a tax point of view you're better off raising horses or cattle than children."

- Congresswoman Patricia R. Schroeder

MEDICAL EXPENSE

Medical expenses can be deducted for you, your spouse, and your dependents for expenses related to the diagnosis, treatment, or prevention of disease, after meeting a deduction threshold based on your income level. In order to calculate the deduction available to you, total your qualified medical expenses for the tax year, and subtract 7.5% of your adjusted gross income (AGI) from that total. The amount in excess represents the deductible portion of your medical costs. Here's an example:

Sam and Audrey file a joint return and their adjusted gross income is $100,000. They incurred $10,000 of medical expenses not reimbursed by health insurance. Their tax deductible medical expenses would be computed as follows:

Total out-of-pocket medical expenses	$10,000
Less 7.5% of AGI ($100,000 x 7.5%)	($7,500)
Deductible medical expenses	**$2,500**

To qualify for this deduction, the expenses must be for the diagnosis, treatment, or prevention of disease.

Expenses incurred for treatments that are generally beneficial to your health (such as vitamins, a health club membership, or a vacation), are not doctor-prescribed (such as over-the-counter medications and band-aids), or are purely cosmetic (such as hair replacement or breast enhancements), are generally not eligible for this deduction.

MEDICAL EXPENSE cont'd

In addition to direct payments for medical care, qualified expenses include long-term health care services, health insurance premiums, and transportation that facilitates medical care.

Tax deductible medical expenses can not already be covered by insurance, a civilian employer, the Department of Veteran Affairs, or other government programs.

A limited tax deduction is available for travel expenses incurred while accompanying a sick child to a treatment facility. Also, the cost of qualified childcare that enables you to receive medical treatment may be deductible in the form of a tax credit if documentation requirements are met.

MEDICAL TRAVEL *See Medical Expense*

The cost of travel to see doctors, fill prescriptions, obtain treatment, attend AA meetings, and attend medical conferences may be a tax deductible expense. Deductible expenses include bus, cab, or train fare, ambulance hire, car use, and lodging to receive outpatient care at a licensed facility. Qualified medical travel costs can be deducted as medical expenses after reaching the required threshold of 7.5% of your AGI.

MEDICARE *See Medical Expense*

Medicare Part A premiums are not tax deductible if you are already covered by Social Security or you are a government employee who paid Medicare tax. Qualified supplemental programs, including Part B premiums, are tax deductible. Qualified Medicare and supplemental premium costs are tax deductible if your medical expenses have reached the deduction threshold of 7.5% of your AGI.

MEDIGAP *See Medical Expense*

Supplemental Medicare insurance premiums are tax deductible subject to the 7.5% AGI threshold for medical expense deductions

MEMBERSHIP FEES

Membership in a club run for social or recreational purposes is not tax deductible even if its use is business-related. The cost of entertaining business associates at the club may be tax deductible as a qualified business expenditure, and is treated as a miscellaneous expense, subject to the 2% AGI threshold, after applying the 50% limit to meal costs. Self-employed individuals can deduct this expense directly from self-employment income, after applying the 50% limit to meal costs.

MISCELLANEOUS EXPENSE

A miscellaneous expense is a tax deductible expense that does not fall into the category of medical or dental, taxes, interest, casualty or theft loss, or charitable contribution. Qualified miscellaneous expenses are unreimbursed costs most often associated with revenue-producing activities such as a hobby, investments, or your job. In order to calculate the deduction available to you, total your qualified miscellaneous expenses for the tax year, and then subtract 2% of your adjusted gross income (AGI) from that total. The remainder represents the deductible portion of your miscellaneous expenses. Generally the 2% threshold is applied after any other deduction limits, if applicable.

MORTGAGE INTEREST

The interest on the first $1,000,000 borrowed to buy, build, or improve your primary and second home is deductible as home acquisition debt. Home mortgage interest for up to two residences is tax deductible. A portion of home mortgage interest can be allocated to a qualified home office based on the percentage of the home that is used for business.

MOTIVATIONAL TAPES, CDs, & BOOKS

Materials purchased that directly motivate you in the performance of your work-related duties are tax deductible. These costs are treated as a miscellaneous expense, subject to the 2% AGI threshold. Self-employed individuals can deduct this expense directly from self-employment income.

MOVING EXPENSES

Job-related moving expenses are tax deductible, subject to requirements of workplace distance and length of employment. Moving costs can be deducted as an adjustment to gross income. Moving expenses are not deductible if you are relocating to start your first job after completing your education, or if you are relocating because of retirement.

MUSIC *See Home Office*

The cost of a music system in a qualified home office may be tax deductible, along with the cost of CDs, satellite radio, and similar products and services. To qualify for this deduction, the system must not be lavish or extravagant for its circumstances. These costs are treated as a miscellaneous expense subject to the 2% AGI threshold. Self-employed individuals can deduct this expense directly from self-employment income.

•N•O•

NAVAJO HEALING CEREMONY

See Medical Expense

The cost of a Navajo healing ceremony may be tax deductible if your medical expenses have reached the required threshold of 7.5% of your AGI.

NEWSLETTERS & NEWSPAPERS

Newspapers, newsletters, and other publications are tax deductible if they are related to work, personal investments, an income-producing hobby, or a job search. Online newsletter subscriptions may also be deducted. For employees, these costs are treated as a miscellaneous expense subject to the 2% AGI threshold. Self-employed individuals can deduct this expense directly from self-employment income.

NICOTINE GUM & NICOTINE PATCHES

Nicotine patches and nicotine gum are not tax deductible.

"Death and taxes and childbirth! There's never any convenient time for any of them."

- Scarlett O'Hara

NURSING *See Medical Expense*

Nursing care (and the associated costs) for yourself, a spouse, or a dependent may be tax deductible if the nursing care is necessary for you to earn income and your medical expenses have reached the required threshold of 7.5% of your AGI. Wages, board, and employment taxes are deductible for at-home nursing and nursing aides, subject to documentation requirements.

NURSING HOME *See Medical Expense*

The cost of nursing homes, convalescent homes, and sanitariums for the elderly and infirm may be tax deductible if your medical expenses have reached the required threshold of 7.5% of your AGI. The cost may be wholly deductible if entry to the facility is at the direction of a doctor, or confinement at the facility is primarily for the treatment of a specific ailment. If confinement is not primarily for the purpose of medical treatment, then the portion of the fees covering meals and lodging is excluded from the deduction.

NUTRITIONAL SUPPLEMENTS

Nutritional supplements, herbal supplements, and vitamins used to improve general health or appearance are not tax deductible, unless they are prescribed by a doctor for the treatment, cure, or prevention of disease. When prescribed, they are a medical expense, subject to the 7.5% AGI threshold.

OBSTETRICIAN *See Medical Expense*

It's getting to where even the patience of the taxpayer is being taxed.

OFFICE SUPPLIES

The home use of office supplies is a tax deductible expense if they are utilized in work-related activities, investment activities, income-producing hobbies, or volunteer work for a qualified charity. Office supplies used in the course of business or in a qualified home office are also tax deductible if they are not reimbursed by your employer. Qualified office supply costs can be deducted as a miscellaneous expense, subject to the 2% AGI threshold. Self-employed individuals can deduct this expense directly from self-employment income.

OPHTHALMOLOGIST/OPTICIAN/OPTOMETRIST

See Medical Expense

ORTHOTICS AND ORTHOPEDIC SHOES

See Medical Expense

The cost of doctor-prescribed orthotics and orthopedic shoes in excess of the cost of regular shoes is tax deductible. The premium paid for specialized footwear may be tax deductible if your medical expenses have reached the required threshold of 7.5% of your AGI.

OVER-THE-COUNTER MEDICATION

See Medical Expense

Over-the-counter medications not doctor-prescribed are not tax deductible. If a medication has been doctor-prescribed, its cost may be tax deductible if your medical expenses have reached the required threshold of 7.5% of your AGI.

P

PAPER GOODS *See Office Supplies*

The home use of printer and fax paper, notebooks, and other paper goods is a tax deductible expense if they are utilized in work-related activities, investment activities, income-producing hobbies, or volunteer work for a qualified charity. Paper goods used in the course of business or in a qualified home office are also tax deductible if they are not reimbursed by your employer. Qualified office supply costs can be deducted as a miscellaneous expense, subject to the 2% AGI threshold. Self-employed individuals can deduct this expense directly from self-employment income.

PARENTAL SUPPORT *See Exemptions*

Support provided to a parent or a stepparent may entitle you to claim them as a dependent resulting in a tax deduction in the form of an exemption. In order to qualify for this deduction, you must provide more than half of your parent or stepparent's support including food, lodging, medical expenses, and education. Your parent or stepparent is not required to live with you in order to be eligible for this deduction. This deduction is subject to restrictions and limitations based on the dependent's income.

"The hardest thing to understand in the world is the income tax."

-Albert Einstein

PARKING

Business-related parking fees or parking costs incurred while engaged in work-related activities, investment activities, income-producing hobbies, or volunteer work for a qualified charity are tax deductible, if not reimbursed by your employer. Parking costs are typically categorized as a miscellaneous expense, subject to the 2% AGI threshold. Self-employed individuals can deduct this expense directly from self-employment income. The cost to park your car while at your regular place of business is a nondeductible commuting expense.

PARKING TICKET

You may not deduct the cost of fines that have been imposed for breaking the law.

PARTIES *See Entertaining*

Parties given to entertain business associates are tax deductible if the event directly relates to the conducting of business, or precedes or follows a business discussion. This includes gatherings held at entertainment, sporting, or recreational facilities. Eligible associates include established and prospective employees, clients, agents, partners, and professional service providers such as bankers and accountants. To qualify for this deduction, the party can not be lavish or extravagant, and most deductions will be limited to 50% of the cost. Seasonal parties for coworkers and employees may be fully deductible.

PASSPORT

The cost of obtaining a passport is tax deductible if it enables tax deductible forms of travel, including travel related to your job, medical treatment, a job search, charitable activity, or education, subject to the criteria and limitations of the applicable deduction based on the intended use of the passport.

PENALTIES

A penalty charged for the early payoff of a home mortgage is treated as tax deductible interest. Interest or principal forfeited as a penalty for the early withdrawal of funds from a time deposit account may also be tax deductible as an adjustment to gross income. Tax-related penalties imposed by the IRS, or any charges imposed for breaking the law, are not tax deductible.

PENS & PENCILS *See Office Supplies*

The home use of pens, pencils, and other writing instruments is a tax deductible expense if they are utilized in work-related activities, investment activities, income-producing hobbies, or volunteer work for a qualified charity. Pens and pencils used in a qualified home office are tax deductible subject to the 2% AGI threshold for employee expenses. Self-employed individuals can deduct this expense directly from self-employment income.

PERSONAL DIGITAL ASSISTANT (PDA) *See Equipment*

PETS

Expenses associated with the purchase and maintenance of house pets are not tax deductible. Dog tag and licensing fees are not deductible. Boarding your pet during business travel is not a tax deductible expense. The expenses associated with guide dogs or other animals used by visually impaired or other physically impaired persons are deductible.

"It is the duty of a good shepherd to shear his sheep, not to skin them."

- Tiberius Caesar

PHOTOCOPYING

Photocopying is a tax deductible expense if utilized in work-related activities, investment activities, income-producing hobbies, or volunteer work for a qualified charity, if not reimbursed by your employer. Photocopying costs incurred in a qualified home office are tax deductible subject to the 2% AGI threshold for employee expenses. Self-employed individuals can deduct this expense directly from self-employment income.

PHYSICAL THERAPY *See Medical Expense*

PLANTS *See Home Office*

The cost of houseplants to decorate a qualified home office may be tax deductible. To qualify for this deduction, the decorations must not be lavish or extravagant for the circumstances. The unreimbursed cost for employees is treated as a miscellaneous expense subject to the 2% AGI threshold. Self-employed individuals can deduct this expense directly from gross income. A home gardening or landscaping service that does not demonstrate your product line or service offerings is not tax deductible even if you maintain a qualified home office.

PODIATRIST/CHIROPODIST *See Medical Expense*

"The only difference between death and taxes is that death doesn't get worse every time Congress meets."

- Will Rogers

POINTS

You generally can not deduct the full amount of points, origination fees, and related costs paid to obtain a mortgage or home improvement loan in the year paid unless the following is true: your loan is secured by your primary residence, the points paid conform to lending practices in your area, the points were not paid in place of amounts that ordinarily are stated separately on the settlement statement (e.g., appraisal fees, inspection fees, title fees, attorney fees, and property taxes), you use the cash method of accounting (claiming income and expenses in the year they occur), and the funds you provided at or before closing, plus any points the seller paid, were at least as much as the points charged.

The funds you provided do not have to have been applied to the points. They can include a down payment, an escrow deposit, earnest money, and other funds you paid at or before closing. You can not have borrowed these funds from your lender or mortgage broker. You must use your loan to buy, build, or improve your main home, and the points must have been computed as a percentage of the principal amount of the mortgage.

Qualified points must appear on your settlement statement as points charged for the mortgage. You may be entitled to deduct points paid by the seller if you subtract that amount from the cost basis of the house.

A portion of home mortgage interest can be allocated to the home office based on the percentage of the home used for business. When points and similar fees are allocated to a home office or a second home, the deduction is generally spread out over the life of the loan.

POLITICAL CONTRIBUTIONS

You can not deduct contributions to a political candidate, a political campaign, or a political party

POSTAGE

Postage and shipping costs are tax deductible if incurred while performing revenue-producing activities such as your job, investments, or a hobby, subject to the 2% AGI threshold for miscellaneous expenses. Self-employed individuals can deduct this expense directly from self-employment income. These costs are also tax deductible if incurred though qualified tax-exempt activities such as educational or charitable pursuits, a job search, or certain legal activities.

PREPAYMENT PENALTIES

Penalties charged for the early payoff of mortgage or home equity loans are treated as mortgage interest and are tax deductible.

PRESCRIPTION DRUGS *See Medical Expense*

Drugs and medications requiring a prescription may be tax deductible if your medical expenses have reached the required threshold of 7.5% of your AGI. Insulin costs may be deducted without a prescription. Over-the-counter medications not doctor-prescribed are not tax deductible.

PRESENTATION MATERIALS

The cost of presentation materials, including photocopying, related to your job, job search, job-related education, investments, or income-producing hobby may be tax deductible, subject to the 2% AGI threshold for miscellaneous expenses. Self-employed individuals can deduct this expense directly from self-employment income.

PRINTER *See Equipment*

The expense incurred to purchase a computer printer, as well as related supplies and accessories, may be tax deductible. The cost of the printer may be depreciated or deducted in the year of purchase or the year in which the printer is placed in service. There is a limit on the dollar amount of assets that can be expensed in the first year. Your income level may limit the amount of the deduction. Tax deductible business uses include printers purchased to monitor investments, for use in a revenue-producing hobby, and for use in a qualified home office. Printers and other equipment purchased for the convenience of your employer or as a requirement of your employment are tax deductible if your employer does not reimburse the cost. Generally, work-related printers and accessories will be treated as a miscellaneous expense, subject to the 2% AGI threshold. Self-employed individuals can deduct this expense directly from self-employment income.

PROFESSIONAL ACCREDITATION FEES

Professional accreditation fees, including certification and licensing fees, are not tax deductible if you have not been previously employed in the profession. Renewing or extending an accreditation, certification, or license in your current field is tax deductible. Licensing and regulatory fees paid to state or local governments are tax deductible. If job-related, these costs are treated as a miscellaneous expense, subject to the 2% AGI threshold. Self-employed individuals can deduct this expense directly from self-employment income.

PROFESSIONAL ASSOCIATION DUES

Dues paid to professional associations and unions are tax deductible if membership is an ordinary and necessary work expense. This includes membership in chambers of commerce, boards of trade, real estate boards, and similar organizations where membership can help you carry out the duties of your job. If job-related, these costs are treated as a miscellaneous expense subject to the 2% AGI threshold. Self-employed individuals can deduct this expense directly from self-employment income.

PROPERTY TAX

City, town, county, and school district taxes paid on any property you own are deductible on your federal tax return. Charges such as fire or sewer taxes may also be deducted if the charge is based on value rather than usage. To calculate the amount of your property tax that is a tax deductible business expense, multiply your property tax by the percentage of your home that is used for business.

PSYCHOLOGIST

See Medical Expense

Licensed psychologist fees may be tax deductible if your medical expenses have reached the required threshold of 7.5% of your AGI. To qualify for this deduction, the expenses must be for the diagnosis, treatment, or prevention of a disease.

PUBLIC BROADCASTING STATION

See Charitable Contributions

A contribution to a public broadcasting station is tax deductible. If you receive a book, CD, or other gift for your contribution, your deduction is limited to the portion in excess of the value of the gift.

·R·

RAFFLE TICKET

The cost of a raffle ticket or other game of chance that is purchased from a charitable organization is not a charitable contribution and may not be deducted.

RAMPS *See Medical Expense*

The installation of ramps for wheelchair access or other medically-necessary reasons is tax deductible to the extent that it does not increase your home's value, and is subject to the conditions and limitations of the medical expense deduction. Additional costs relating to architecture and aesthetics may not be deducted.

RECREATIONAL VEHICLES *See Automobile Expense*

A recreational vehicle used in your job or business is treated as any other automobile for tax purposes if its use is deemed ordinary and necessary to the nature of the work.

REFINANCING *See Mortgage Interest/Points*

The interest charged to refinance a mortgage or home equity loan is deductible. If excess proceeds are applied to personal debt or expenses, then that portion of the loan is not deductible. Depending on funding criteria and use of the funds provided, points associated with the new loan may be tax deductible, but the deduction might have to be spread out over the life of the loan.

REMEDIAL READING *See Medical Expense*

Fees paid to a doctor-recommended tutor for remedial reading may be tax deductible if your medical expenses have reached the required threshold of 7.5% of your AGI. The cost of tutoring a learning disabled child is a qualified medical expense if the disability is caused by mental or physical impairments, including nervous system disorders.

RENT

If you are renting your primary residence and operate a qualified home office from your home, a portion of the rent based on the percentage of the home used for business can be allocated to the home office. Non-office workspaces eligible for the rent expense include studios, barns, garages, greenhouses, meeting rooms, and storage areas. If you are not self-employed, this deduction is treated as an unreimbursed employee expense and is tax deductible after reaching the required threshold of 2% of your AGI. Self-employed individuals can deduct this expense directly from self-employment income. If you own your home, you can not charge rent to your home-based business.

RENTAL PROPERTY EXPENSES

The ordinary and necessary expenses incurred to manage, conserve, and maintain rental property that you own are tax deductible, including the cost of travel to and from the rental property. If the rental property is also used for personal purposes, you may be eligible to claim a full mortgage interest deduction. If you exceed the allowable number of personal days or exceed restrictions on the size of the mortgage, your mortgage interest deduction may be prorated accordingly, and the deduction may be limited. Your deductible rental loss may be limited by your level of activity in the rental business or your investment in the property.

REPAIRS *See Capital Improvements/Rental Property*

The cost of repairs to your home is not generally tax deductible. If you maintain a home office within your home, you can deduct the cost of repairs to the workspace. Significant repairs are considered capital improvements in that they extend the life of the asset. If a repair benefits the entire house (such as repairing a central air conditioning system), a portion of the costs can be allocated to the home office, based on the percentage of the home used for business, and can be depreciated. The cost of repairs to revenue-producing rental property is tax deductible if the repairs are ordinary and necessary to maintain the property.

RESUME *See Job Search Expense*

All costs associated with the preparation and distribution of resumes for a qualified job search may be tax deductible. The search must be within your present field, without a substantial break between your last employment and the job search. Qualified expenses may be deducted even if the job search does not lead to a new job. These costs are treated as a miscellaneous expense, subject to the 2% AGI threshold. Recent college graduates with no experience or internships in their prospective field are not eligible for these deductions.

RETIREMENT SAVINGS

Contributions made to an IRA, 401(k), Keogh Plan, Self Employment Pension Plan (SEP), Corporate Retirement Plan (ERISA), and other qualified retirement savings plans are treated as deferrals to taxable income. While not a true tax deduction, the effect of the deferment of taxes has the same impact on current income as a tax deduction.

·S·

SAFES & SAFE DEPOSIT BOXES

The rental fee on a safe deposit box is a tax deductible investment expense. The cost of installing a safe in your home or office is also tax deductible. These costs are treated as a miscellaneous expense subject to the 2% AGI threshold. Self-employed individuals can deduct this expense directly from self-employment income.

SAFETY GLASSES *See Clothing and Uniforms*

Safety glasses and goggles are tax deductible if they serve a work-related function, are protective in nature, or are not adaptable for everyday wear. If not reimbursed by your employer, the cost is treated as a miscellaneous expense, subject to the 2% AGI threshold. Self-employed individuals can deduct this expense directly from self-employment income.

SALES TAX

You may elect to deduct state and local sales taxes in place of the deduction for state and local income taxes on your federal tax return. You can deduct your actual sales tax expense (which requires extensive documentation), or use the IRS-provided estimates based on income and exemptions. Sales tax paid during the tax year on major purchases such as cars, boats, airplanes, and home-building materials can be added to the IRS-provided estimates.

SEASON TICKETS *See Entertaining*

Hosting business associates at recreational or entertainment events is tax deductible if it directly relates to the conducting of business, or precedes or follows a business discussion. The deduction is limited to 50% of the prorated season expense, and each occasion within a season is treated as a separate deduction. Entertaining is treated as a miscellaneous expense, subject to the 2% AGI threshold after applying the 50% limit to the costs. Self-employed individuals can deduct this expense, after applying the 50% limit, directly from self-employment income.

SECURITY

The costs associated with installing and maintaining a security system, security devices, or a security monitoring service are tax deductible. The deduction is allocated to the home office at a rate based on the business use of the home, or may be wholly deductible if the system provides security exclusively for a separate business structure, subject to the 2% AGI threshold for miscellaneous expenses. Self-employed individuals can deduct this expense directly from self-employment income. If a large investment is made in systems and equipment, those items should be depreciated as equipment expenditures.

6,000,000,000

The number of hours Americans spend preparing tax forms and record keeping to comply with IRS requirements.

SELF-EMPLOYMENT TAX

If you are self-employed, one half of your self-employment tax is deductible as an adjustment to gross income.

SEMINARS *See Education*

The costs to attend a job-related training session or seminar are tax deductible if not reimbursed by your employer. The deduction includes course registration fees, books, and other related materials. To qualify for the deduction, the class can not be taken to enhance personal growth or to acquire skills that lead to a new line of work, but must maintain or enhance the skills required by your current position. These costs are treated as a miscellaneous expense, subject to the 2% AGI deduction threshold. Self-employed individuals can deduct this expense directly from self-employment income.

SEP *See Retirement Savings*

SHOE SHINE *See Clothing and Uniforms*

The cost of shoe shines, polish, and similar items and services used in the maintenance of your professional uniform is a tax deductible miscellaneous expense subject to the 2% AGI threshold. Self-employed individuals can deduct this expense directly from self-employment income.

SMOKING CESSATION PROGRAM

See Medical Expense/Nicotine Gum

A qualified smoking cessation program may be tax deductible if your medical expenses have reached the required threshold of 7.5% of your AGI. The program does not have to be prescribed by a doctor to qualify for this deduction. Non-prescription aids such as gum and patches are not deductible.

SOFTWARE *See Equipment/Home Office*

Software purchases may be tax deductible as a depreciable asset with a useful life of more than one year. The cost of the software may be depreciated or deducted in the year of purchase or the year placed in service. There is a limit on the dollar amount of assets that can be written off in the first year. Your income level may limit the amount of the deduction. Included in this deduction is software purchased to monitor investments, for use in a revenue-producing hobby, and or for use in a qualified home office.

Software purchased for the convenience of your employer or as a requirement of your employment is tax deductible if your employer does not reimburse the cost. Qualified job-related software costs and depreciation can be deducted as a miscellaneous expense, subject to the 2% AGI threshold.

The cost of software employed in volunteer duties is treated as a charitable contribution and may be tax deductible to a maximum of 50% of your AGI.

SPORTING EVENT *See Entertaining*

Hosting business associates at a sporting event is tax deductible if it directly relates to the conducting of business, or precedes or follows a business discussion.

Eligible associates include established and prospective employees, clients, agents, partners, and professional service providers such as bankers and accountants. The deduction is limited to 50% of the expense, and for employees is further subject to the 2% AGI threshold for miscellaneous expenses, and may not include the cost of membership at a golf club or country club. Self-employed individuals can deduct this expense after applying the 50% limit, directly from self-employment income.

SPORTING EVENT cont'd

When golfing in a charity golf tournament or outing, the greens fees and value of other benefits, such as beverages and dining, must be subtracted from the event cost to determine the tax deductible portion of your contribution.

SPOUSE INCLUSION *See Entertaining*

If entertaining business associates as a couple, the cost of including your spouse, partner, or significant other is tax deductible subject to the requirements and limitations of qualified entertainment expenses.

STATE INCOME TAX

State income taxes are tax deductible on your federal tax return. You may elect to deduct state and local general sales tax in place of the income tax deduction. This option is available for all filers, but especially recommended for residents of states without income taxes. You may deduct actual sales tax paid or an estimate based on the IRS optional sales tax tables.

STATIONERY *See Office Supplies*

The home use of stationery is a tax deductible expense if it is used in investment activities, income-producing hobbies, or volunteer work for a qualified charity. Stationery and other supplies used in a qualified home office are tax deductible, subject to the 2% AGI threshold for miscellaneous expenses. Self-employed individuals can deduct this expense directly from self-employment income.

• A FINE IS A TAX FOR DOING WRONG.

STOLEN CAR *See Casualty Loss*

The cost of a personal car that is lost or damaged due to theft is tax deductible if not covered by insurance. The loss is measured by the lesser of the decrease in fair market value of the car or your cost of the car. The deduction is derived by reducing the loss by $100 and then by 10% of AGI. The loss can not be the result of neglect or willful misconduct on your part.

STUDENT LOAN INTEREST

A limited portion of the interest paid on a qualified student loan is tax deductible as an adjustment to gross income on page 1 of your 1040.

SUBSCRIPTIONS

Subscriptions to publications may be deducted if they are related to work, personal investments, or a job search. Qualified online subscriptions may also be deducted. In the case of prepaid multi-year subscriptions, you can only deduct the subscription costs associated with the current tax year. These costs are treated as a miscellaneous expense subject to the 2% AGI threshold. Self-employed individuals can deduct this expense directly from self-employment income.

SUNGLASSES *See Medical Expense*

The cost of prescription sunglasses may be tax deductible if your medical expenses have reached the required threshold of 7.5% of your AGI.

• A TAX IS A FINE FOR DOING WELL.

.T.

TAX BOOKS

Tax guides and workbooks are tax deductible, including this one!

TAX PENALTY

Penalties for late or insufficient tax payments are not tax deductible.

TAX PREPARATION

Costs associated with the preparation, filing, and auditing of both your federal and state tax returns are tax deductible. This includes workbooks and guides, software, filing fees, tax preparer fees, and accountant fees. These costs are treated as a miscellaneous expense subject to the 2% AGI threshold. Self-employed individuals can deduct this expense directly from self-employment income.

TAXES

State, city, and county income taxes are tax deductible on your federal tax return. Property taxes paid to a city, town, county, or school district are tax deductible. Fire or sewer taxes are also tax deductible if based on value rather than usage. There are no limits on the number of homes for which you can claim this deduction. Occupation tax charged at a flat rate, and state or local per capita taxes may not be deducted. If you pay the taxes of an individual who is not your child or dependent, those tax payments are not tax deductible to you. They are considered to be a nondeductible gift.

TAXES cont'd

Taxes paid to other governments may be deductible in the form of a tax credit. Taxes imposed by governments with which the United States does not maintain diplomatic relations, or that have been identified as providing support to terrorists, will not result in a tax credit or deduction.

TELEPHONE

Telephone costs, including internet connectivity, can be a tax deductible expense if they are related to a job search, or an income-producing activity such as investments or hobbies. Deductible expenses may include equipment such as cell phones and pagers, as well as usage charges for land lines and cellular phones. Job-related expenditures may also be deducted if not reimbursed by your employer. These costs are treated as a miscellaneous expense subject to the 2% AGI threshold. The basic service charge for your personal line (land line or cellular) must be excluded from this deduction. Self-employed individuals can deduct this expense directly from self-employment income.

TELEVISION ADAPTER *See Medical Expense*

The cost of a closed-caption television adapter is a tax deductible medical expense for a hearing-impaired taxpayer or dependent, subject to the medical expense deduction threshold of 7.5% of your AGI.

"What is the difference between a taxidermist and a tax collector? The taxidermist takes only your skin."

- Mark Twain

TEMPORARY WORK ASSIGNMENT EXPENSES

The commuting cost to travel between home and a temporary work assignment is tax deductible. If the distance is too great or your ongoing presence necessitates temporary housing, the associated living expenses can also be tax deductible. Deductible expenses include transportation costs, hotels, 50% of meals, telephone and internet access charges, laundry, cleaning, and related tips. Business travel not fully or partially reimbursed by your employer is tax deductible as a miscellaneous expense, subject to the 2% AGI threshold. Self-employed individuals can deduct this expense directly from self-employment income.

TIPS

Tips paid to service personnel such as drivers, porters, parking attendants, and waiters may be tax deductible if the expense is associated with qualified tax deductible activity and tipping is ordinary and expected. These costs are treated as a miscellaneous expense subject to the 2% AGI threshold. Self-employed individuals can deduct this expense directly from self-employment income.

TITLE INSURANCE

Title insurance for the purchase of your home is not tax deductible, but can result in a tax reduction when you sell your home by adding to its cost basis.

TOLLS *See Automobile Expense*

If you own or lease a car and use it in your job or business, then the operating cost can be deducted from taxes. The deduction can be based on either miles driven or the actual costs of maintaining and operating the car. Toll costs are deductible if the deduction is based on actual costs.

TONER *See Office Supplies*

TOOLS *See Equipment*

The cost incurred to purchase tools specific to your work or a revenue-producing hobby is tax deductible. If the tools have a useful life of more than one year, the expense may be depreciated or deducted in the year of purchase based on cost and business use. Your income level may limit the deduction. Tools purchased for the convenience of your employer or are a requirement of your employment are tax deductible if your employer does not reimburse the cost. Qualified tool costs and depreciation can be deducted as a miscellaneous expense, subject to the 2% AGI threshold. Self-employed individuals can deduct this expense directly from self-employment income. The cost of tools employed in volunteer duties is treated as a charitable contribution and may be tax deductible to a maximum of 50% of your AGI.

TOOTH WHITENING

Tooth whitening is not a tax deductible medical expense if performed for cosmetic purposes, such as to correct discoloration due to aging. It is tax deductible if it is performed to correct a deformity due to illness, injury, or a congenital abnormality.

TRADE SHOW *See Business Travel*

TRAINING *See Job-Related Education*

TRAVEL EXPENSE *See Business Travel*

TRUSTEE FEES

Payments of custodial or trustee fees to maintain an IRA account are tax deductible. The fees can not be debited from the IRA account, but must be paid directly to the custodian or trustee in order to qualify for this deduction.

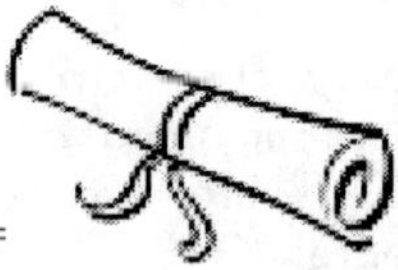

TUITION

Tuition, including course registration fees, books, materials, and related supplies, may be a tax deductible expense if it is for job-related education that is not reimbursed by your employer, or for doctor-recommended special education for a child with learning disabilities caused by mental or physical impairments.

A limited adjustment to gross income can also be taken for a portion of college, graduate school, or vocational school tuition and fees for yourself, your spouse, or your dependents. This deduction is available whether you finance the education costs through loans or your own savings. Payments must be made to a qualified institution, and can not be applied toward other tuition deduction programs such as the Hope credit or the Lifetime Learning credit for higher education.

Tuition payments made from the proceeds of a tax-free scholarship, a tax-free educational savings account, or the excludable interest earned from U.S. savings bonds can not be applied toward the tuition deduction. Tuition paid by a grandparent or another party, or payments made under a divorce decree directly to the educational facility result in a tax deduction for the student, unless the student can be claimed as a dependent by the other taxpayer.

·V W·

UNEMPLOYMENT INSURANCE

Voluntary contributions to an unemployment benefit fund through a union or a privately held fund are not tax deductible. If your state requires payments to a state unemployment fund, those payments are deductible.

UNIFORMS *See Clothing and Uniforms*

Work-related clothing and uniform costs may be tax deductible. In order to qualify for this deduction, the clothing must be required for your job and not be adaptable for everyday wear. Costumes or articles of clothing that display an employer's logo or advertising may be deductible. The unreimbursed cost of purchasing, cleaning, and maintaining job-related clothing and uniforms may be deducted as a miscellaneous expense, subject to the 2% AGI threshold. Self-employed individuals can deduct this expense directly from self-employment income.

UNION DUES

Dues paid to a union or professional association may be tax deductible as a qualified business expense if membership is necessary or beneficial to your job. These costs are treated as a miscellaneous expense subject to the 2% AGI threshold. Self-employed individuals can deduct this expense directly from self-employment income.

UNPAID BALANCE ON A LOAN

The unpaid balance from a personal loan made to another individual may be tax deductible. To qualify for the deduction, the loan must truly be uncollectible, can not be construed as a gift, and must not violate state usury laws. An unpaid balance owed to you by a political party or committee does not qualify for this deduction. Unpaid child support is not tax deductible as a bad debt.

UNREIMBURSED EMPLOYEE EXPENSE

An expense common to your trade or business but which is not reimbursed by your employer may be tax deductible. In order to qualify, the expense must be appropriate and helpful to your work, or be required as a condition of your employment or for the convenience of your employer. This includes unreimbursed expenses for business-related travel and education, as well as the expenses associated with a home office. In most cases, the costs are deductible as a miscellaneous expense after you have met the expense threshold of 2% of your AGI.

USED CLOTHING DONATIONS *See Charitable Contributions*

The value of used clothing is tax deductible if donated to an IRS-approved, tax-exempt nonprofit organization. The deduction should be based on the fair market value of the used clothing. An appraiser should verify the tax deduction taken for large donations, such as furs or designer gowns. For most charitable donations, the maximum you can deduct in one tax year is limited to 50% of your AGI. In the event of larger donations, the portion of the deduction in excess of the cap can be carried forward to offset income in the following tax year.

UTILITIES *See Home Office*

The cost of the utilities necessary to operate a qualified home office is tax deductible. Usage is allocated to the home office at a rate based on the business use of the home, or at a greater rate if a high level of utility usage can be attributed to the functioning of the office. Job-related home office expenses are tax deductible after reaching the required miscellaneous expense threshold of 2% of your AGI. Self-employed individuals can deduct this expense directly from self-employment income.

VACATION HOME *See Rental Property*

Real estate taxes and home mortgage interest associated with a vacation home are tax deductible expenses if the home is reserved solely for personal use. Taxes, interest, utilities, and other expenses necessary to maintain a vacation home that generates rental income may be partly or wholly deductible. The deduction may be limited by the allocation between personal use and rental use of the vacation home, and the criteria, restrictions, and expense threshold of the deduction will vary by expense category.

VANDALISM *See Casualty Loss*

A loss of personal property due to vandalism is tax deductible if not covered by insurance. The loss can not be the result of neglect or willful misconduct on your part. The deduction is derived by reducing the loss by $100 and then by 10% of AGI.

VETERANS ORGANIZATIONS

See Charitable Contributions

Contributions to veterans groups are tax deductible if made to an IRS-approved, tax-exempt nonprofit organization. Large donations require documentation from the receiving organization. For most charitable donations, the maximum you can deduct in one tax year is limited to 50% of your AGI. In the event of larger contributions, the portion of the deduction in excess of the cap can be carried forward to offset income in the following tax year.

VIDEOS *See Education Expense/Office Supplies*

The cost to purchase or rent videos is tax deductible if the expense is related to work, personal investments, a job search, or is a qualified education expense The deduction is subject to the 2% AGI threshold for miscellaneous expenses. Self-employed individuals can deduct this expense directly from self-employment income.

VITAMINS *See Medical Expense*

Vitamins that have been doctor-prescribed to treat a specific condition may be tax deductible if your medical expenses have reached the required threshold of 7.5% of your AGI. Vitamins taken for general health benefits are not deductible.

VOLUNTEER SERVICES

Individuals who volunteer their services to qualified organizations can deduct the costs of their unreimbursed expenses that directly relate to their volunteer activity. These expenses can include travel, equipment, uniforms, and other costs incurred in the performance of volunteer service. The value of time or services is not deductible.

W

WEB SITE DEVELOPMENT, DESIGN, & HOSTING

Web site development, design, and hosting costs can be a tax deductible expense if they are related to a job search or an income-producing activity such as investments or revenue-producing hobbies. Job-related web site expenditures may also be deducted if not reimbursed by your employer. These costs are treated as a miscellaneous expense subject to the 2% AGI threshold. Self-employed individuals can deduct this expense directly from self-employment income.

WEEKEND TRAVEL *See Business Travel*

If a weekend or a holiday falls between business travel days, the expenses associated with staying on site the extra time are tax deductible.

WEIGHT LOSS PROGRAM *See Medical Expense*

The cost of a qualified doctor-prescribed weight loss program, including health club costs, is tax deductible if medically-necessary to treat a specific disease or weight-related condition, such as obesity or high blood pressure. This deduction is available if your medical expenditures have reached the required threshold of 7.5% of your AGI.

WEIGHT TRAINING *See Medical Expense*

The cost of a doctor-prescribed weight training program including the cost of a health club membership is tax deductible if medically-necessary to treat a specific disease or condition. The cost to maintain a fitness level necessary to the performance of your duties may be tax deductible if your job requires strenuous or extraordinary activity on a regular basis. This deduction is available if your medical expenditures have reached the required threshold of 7.5% of your AGI.

WIG *See Medical Expense*

The cost of a wig is a tax deductible medical expense if hair loss is due to illness or treatment and a wig is considered essential to mental health. This deduction is available if your medical expenditures have reached the required threshold of 7.5% of your AGI. Wigs purchased for purely cosmetic reasons are not tax deductible.

WILL PREPARATION

The personal legal expenses associated with the preparation of a will are not tax deductible.

WIND DAMAGE *See Casualty Loss*

A loss to personal property due to tornado, hurricane, or other wind event is tax deductible if not covered by insurance or other disaster relief, subject to the casualty loss rules and limitations.

WITHDRAWAL PENALTY

The penalty imposed for the early withdrawal of funds from savings accounts or other savings vehicles is tax deductible as an adjustment to gross income.

WORK CLOTHES *See Clothing &Uniforms*

Specialized work clothing costs are tax deductible if the items are protective in nature, specially designed, or not adaptable for everyday wear. This deduction includes articles displaying an employer's logo or advertising. The unreimbursed cost of purchasing, cleaning, and maintaining work-related clothing and uniforms may be deducted as well. Work clothes are generally considered a miscellaneous expense, subject to the 2% AGI threshold. Self-employed individuals can deduct this expense directly from self-employment income.

WRISTWATCH

The cost of a wristwatch is not tax deductible even if you are required to know the correct time in order to perform your required duties.

"The ancient Egyptians built elaborate fortresses and tunnels and even posted guards at tombs to stop grave robbers. In today's America, we call that estate planning."

-Congressman Bill Archer

·X·Y·Z·

YARD WORK

A home gardening or landscaping service is not tax deductible (unless you work in the industry and it serves to demonstrate your product line or service offerings), even if you maintain a qualified home office.

YELLOW PAGES AD

Yellow Pages advertising costs may be tax deductible if they are ordinary and necessary to your business and are not reimbursed by your employer. The cost of advertising to promote an income-producing hobby is tax deductible to the extent that it is offset by hobby income.

ZIP DRIVE/ZIP DISKS *See Office Supplies*

ZONING

The costs of zoning permits and filings incurred to construct, maintain, or improve a home office or other work space are tax deductible. The costs must be appropriate to your business. Eligible structures include office, workshop, warehouse, studio, storage, and showroom space.

HOW TO USE THE EXPENSE TRACKERS

We suggest that you begin by taking a quick look through the alphabetized deduction listings to see if anything pops out at you that you hadn't thought of.

If you own or lease a car and use it in your work or other revenue-producing activities, then the cost of operating it can be deducted from taxes.

Maybe you spent money on education, computer equipment, office supplies, advertising, or retained an executive recruiter. All of these are examples of activities that can result in business expense tax deductions. Generally the 2% threshold is applied to business expenses, after any other deduction limits, if applicable.

Hosting business associates at recreational or entertainment events is tax deductible if it directly relates to the conducting of business, or precedes or follows a business discussion.

Generally, 50% of the cost of dining may be tax deductible when it is incurred as a qualified business expense. Meal costs may also be deducted when incurred through tax deductible forms of travel such as charitable, educational, business, medical, or adoption-related travel.

Now that you know what to look out for, you can start accumulating the documentation necessary to claim those deductions. This is not really as daunting as it sounds. It can be as simple as checking your car's mileage and jotting it down in a handy log.

And finally, when April 15th rolls around—itemize. All of these deductions are only available to you if you itemize on your tax return. Don't be seduced by the 1040EZ. Stop missing out on the deductions you are entitled to and start keeping more of the money you earn.

Date • / / VEHICLE •

Destination •

Purpose •

START • ___ _, ___ _. _ MILES DRIVEN

END • ___ _, ___ _. _

Date • / / VEHICLE •

Destination •

Purpose •

START • ___ _, ___ _. _ MILES DRIVEN

END • ___ _, ___ _. _

Date • / / VEHICLE •

Destination •

Purpose •

START • ___ _, ___ _. _ MILES DRIVEN

END • ___ _, ___ _. _

Date • / / VEHICLE •

Destination •

Purpose •

START • ___ _, ___ _. _ MILES DRIVEN

END • ___ _, ___ _. _

MILEAGE TRACKER

Date • / / VEHICLE •

Destination •

Purpose •

START • ___ _, ___ _. _ | MILES DRIVEN

END • ___ _, ___ _. _

Date • / / VEHICLE •

Destination •

Purpose •

START • ___ _, ___ _. _ | MILES DRIVEN

END • ___ _, ___ _. _

Date • / / VEHICLE •

Destination •

Purpose •

START • ___ _, ___ _. _ | MILES DRIVEN

END • ___ _, ___ _. _

Date • / / VEHICLE •

Destination •

Purpose •

START • ___ _, ___ _. _ | MILES DRIVEN

END • ___ _, ___ _. _

Date • / / VEHICLE •

Destination •

Purpose •

START • ___ _, ___ _. _

MILES DRIVEN

END • ___ _, ___ _. _

Date • / / VEHICLE •

Destination •

Purpose •

START • ___ _, ___ _. _

MILES DRIVEN

END • ___ _, ___ _. _

Date • / / VEHICLE •

Destination •

Purpose •

START • ___ _, ___ _. _

MILES DRIVEN

END • ___ _, ___ _. _

Date • / / VEHICLE •

Destination •

Purpose •

START • ___ _, ___ _. _

MILES DRIVEN

END • ___ _, ___ _. _

MILEAGE TRACKER

Date • / / *VEHICLE* •	
Destination •	
Purpose •	
START • ___ _, ___ _. _	*MILES DRIVEN*
END • ___ _, ___ _. _	

Date • / / *VEHICLE* •	
Destination •	
Purpose •	
START • ___ _, ___ _. _	*MILES DRIVEN*
END • ___ _, ___ _. _	

Date • / / *VEHICLE* •	
Destination •	
Purpose •	
START • ___ _, ___ _. _	*MILES DRIVEN*
END • ___ _, ___ _. _	

Date • / / *VEHICLE* •	
Destination •	
Purpose •	
START • ___ _, ___ _. _	*MILES DRIVEN*
END • ___ _, ___ _. _	

Date • / / VEHICLE •	
Destination •	
Purpose •	
START • ___ __, ___ __. _	MILES DRIVEN
END • ___ _, ___ __. _	
Date • / / VEHICLE •	
Destination •	
Purpose •	
START • ___ __, ___ __. _	MILES DRIVEN
END • ___ _, ___ __. _	
Date • / / VEHICLE •	
Destination •	
Purpose •	
START • ___ __, ___ __. _	MILES DRIVEN
END • ___ _, ___ __. _	
Date • / / VEHICLE •	
Destination •	
Purpose •	
START • ___ __, ___ __. _	MILES DRIVEN
END • ___ _, ___ __. _	

MILEAGE TRACKER

Date • / / VEHICLE •

Destination •

Purpose •

START • ___ _, ___ _. _ | MILES DRIVEN

END • ___ _, ___ _. _

Date • / / VEHICLE •

Destination •

Purpose •

START • ___ _, ___ _. _ | MILES DRIVEN

END • ___ _, ___ _. _

Date • / / VEHICLE •

Destination •

Purpose •

START • ___ _, ___ _. _ | MILES DRIVEN

END • ___ _, ___ _. _

Date • / / VEHICLE •

Destination •

Purpose •

START • ___ _, ___ _. _ | MILES DRIVEN

END • ___ _, ___ _. _

DATE	ITEM
/ /	
/ /	
/ /	
/ /	
/ /	
/ /	
/ /	
/ /	
/ /	
/ /	
/ /	
/ /	
/ /	
/ /	
/ /	
/ /	
/ /	
/ /	
/ /	
/ /	
/ /	
/ /	
/ /	
/ /	

UNREIMBURSED BUSINESS EXPENSE

AMOUNT	*PURPOSE*	√
		☐
		☐
		☐
		☐
		☐
		☐
		☐
		☐
		☐
		☐
		☐
		☐
		☐
		☐
		☐
		☐
		☐
		☐
		☐
		☐
		☐
		☐
		☐
		☐

DATE	*ITEM*
/ /	
/ /	
/ /	
/ /	
/ /	
/ /	
/ /	
/ /	
/ /	
/ /	
/ /	
/ /	
/ /	
/ /	
/ /	
/ /	
/ /	
/ /	
/ /	
/ /	
/ /	
/ /	
/ /	
/ /	

UNREIMBURSED BUSINESS EXPENSE

AMOUNT	*PURPOSE*	√
		☐
		☐
		☐
		☐
		☐
		☐
		☐
		☐
		☐
		☐
		☐
		☐
		☐
		☐
		☐
		☐
		☐
		☐
		☐
		☐
		☐
		☐
		☐
		☐

DATE	ITEM
/ /	
/ /	
/ /	
/ /	
/ /	
/ /	
/ /	
/ /	
/ /	
/ /	
/ /	
/ /	
/ /	
/ /	
/ /	
/ /	
/ /	
/ /	
/ /	
/ /	
/ /	
/ /	
/ /	
/ /	

UNREIMBURSED BUSINESS EXPENSE

AMOUNT	*PURPOSE*	√
		☐
		☐
		☐
		☐
		☐
		☐
		☐
		☐
		☐
		☐
		☐
		☐
		☐
		☐
		☐
		☐
		☐
		☐
		☐
		☐
		☐
		☐
		☐
		☐

LOCATION • ______________________ *Date* • / /

Attendees •

Notes •

Total • $ _____

LOCATION • ______________________ *Date* • / /

Attendees •

Notes •

Total • $ _____

LOCATION • ______________________ *Date* • / /

Attendees •

Notes •

Total • $ _____

LOCATION • ______________________ *Date* • / /

Attendees •

Notes •

Total • $ _____

LOCATION • ______________________ *Date* • / /

Attendees •

Notes •

Total • $ _____

LOCATION • ____________________ *Date* • / /

Attendees •

Notes •

Total • $ _____

LOCATION • ____________________ *Date* • / /

Attendees •

Notes •

Total • $ _____

LOCATION • ____________________ *Date* • / /

Attendees •

Notes •

Total • $ _____

LOCATION • ____________________ *Date* • / /

Attendees •

Notes •

Total • $ _____

LOCATION • ____________________ *Date* • / /

Attendees •

Notes •

Total • $ _____

LOCATION • ______________________ *Date* • / /

Attendees •

Notes •

Total • $ _____

LOCATION • ______________________ *Date* • / /

Attendees •

Notes •

Total • $ _____

LOCATION • ______________________ *Date* • / /

Attendees •

Notes •

Total • $ _____

LOCATION • ______________________ *Date* • / /

Attendees •

Notes •

Total • $ _____

LOCATION • ______________________ *Date* • / /

Attendees •

Notes •

Total • $ _____

LOCATION • ____________________ *Date* • / /

Attendees •

Notes •

Total • $ _____

LOCATION • ____________________ *Date* • / /

Attendees •

Notes •

Total • $ _____

LOCATION • ____________________ *Date* • / /

Attendees •

Notes •

Total • $ _____

LOCATION • ____________________ *Date* • / /

Attendees •

Notes •

Total • $ _____

LOCATION • ____________________ *Date* • / /

Attendees •

Notes •

Total • $ _____

LOCATION • ______________________ *Date* • / /

Attendees •

Notes •

Total • $ _____

LOCATION • ______________________ *Date* • / /

Attendees •

Notes •

Total • $ _____

LOCATION • ______________________ *Date* • / /

Attendees •

Notes •

Total • $ _____

LOCATION • ______________________ *Date* • / /

Attendees •

Notes •

Total • $ _____

LOCATION • ______________________ *Date* • / /

Attendees •

Notes •

Total • $ _____

LOCATION • ______________________ *Date* • / /

Attendees •

Notes •

Total • $ _____

LOCATION • ______________________ *Date* • / /

Attendees •

Notes •

Total • $ _____

LOCATION • ______________________ *Date* • / /

Attendees •

Notes •

Total • $ _____

LOCATION • ______________________ *Date* • / /

Attendees •

Notes •

Total • $ _____

LOCATION • ______________________ *Date* • / /

Attendees •

Notes •

Total • $ _____

NOTES

Following is a listing of IRS publications that can assist you in preparing your tax return. Forms and publications can be accessed and downloaded through the IRS web site at www.irs.gov/formspubs. You can request forms and publications to be sent through conventional mail by calling the IRS at 1-800-829-3676.

GENERAL TAX INFORMATION

When, Where, and How to File....Topic 301
Tax Guide for Individuals....Pub. 17
Record Keeping....Pub. 552
Automatic Extension of Time To File....Form 4868
Change of Address....Form 8822

FAMILY TAX MATTERS

Adoption Topics....Tax Topic 607, Form 8839
Children and Dependents....Pub. 503, Pub. 929
Divorce....Topic 406, Topic 452, Pub. 504

SENIORS

Tax Guide for Older Americans....Pub. 554
Tax Guide for Retirees....Pub. 4190

EDUCATION

Work-Related Education....Pub. 508
Higher Education....Pub. 970, Topic 457
Student Loan Interest....Topic 456
Qualified Expenses....Topic 513

HOME OWNERSHIP

First-time Home Owners....Pub. 530
Home Mortgage Interest....Pub. 936
Selling Your Home....Pub. 523
Moving Expenses....Pub. 521
Real Estate Taxes....Pub. 950
Rental Property....Topic 414, Topic 415, Pub. 527

CHARITABLE CONTRIBUTIONS

Qualified Contributions....Pub. 561, Pub. 4303, Pub. 1771, Form 8283
Valuing Property Donations....Pub. 526

SAVING/INVESTING

IRAs.......*Pub. 17, Pub. 590, Topic 428, Topic 451*
Investment Interest.......*Form 4952*

BUSINESS EXPENSES

Qualified Business Expenses.......*Pub. 535*
Business Travel ....*Topic 511*
Business Use of Car.......*Topic 510*
Business Use of Home.......*Pub. 587*
Business Entertaining.......*Topic 512*
Travel.......*Topic 511, Pub. 463*

HOME OFFICE

Business Use of Your Home.......*Pub. 587, Topic 509, Pub. 4035,*
Medical and Dental.......*Pub. 502*

RECORD RETENTION GUIDE

Federal tax returns can generally be subject to audit for up to six years after filing. To comply with the documentation requirements, we suggest that you follow these guidelines for retaining financial documents.

Record — Retention Period

- Federal tax returns.......7+ years
- W2/1099.......7 years
- Home purchase/sale/improvements.......duration of ownership + 7 years
- Expense logs.......7 years
- Banking records (statements, transaction slips, cancelled checks).......7 years
- Investment records (year-end statements, transaction documentation).......duration of ownership of investment vehicle + 7 years
- Home/property ownership documents.......duration of ownership + 7 years
- Home improvements.......duration of ownership + 7 years
- Home repairs.......warranty period
- Retirement plan/IRA/pension (statements, annual reports, transaction documentation).......permanent
- Loan records.......life of loan + 7 years
- Insurance policies.......permanent

Other Titles In This Series

Tax Deductions A to Z™

Tax Deductions A to Z™ for Clergy

Tax Deductions A to Z™ for Educators

Tax Deductions A to Z™ for Fire, Police & EMT

Tax Deductions A to Z™ for Freelancer and Contractors

Tax Deductions A to Z™ for Health Care Professionals

Tax Deductions A to Z™ for Military & Reservists

Tax Deductions A to Z™ for Sales Professionals

Tax Deductions A to Z™ for Trades People & Union Members

Tax Deductions A to Z™ for Writers, Artists and Performers

Tax Deductions A to Z™ Log Book